CW00498599

Hong Kong

Select

contents

Hong Kong overview

Often compared to Manhattan on account of its urban skyscraper-scape, Hong Kong is at first glance quite like a modern Western city; but it has distinct Chinese characteristics. Take a few turns off its gleaming, dynamic downtown streets, and you'll get an idea of how much tradition is ingrained.

In the shadows of tower blocks, colourful temples and street shrines bear continually replenished offerings of fresh fruit and burning incense sticks and coils. Teahouses and compact noodle shops are abuzz with as much activity as the more recent additions of coffee-houses and juice-bar chains.

Working Hong Kongers may like their designer togs – and there are malls full of them – but every neighbourhood is home to practitioners of traditional Chinese medicine, who are kept as busy by young executive types as they are by the older generation.

While Hong Kong is home to the world's most densely populated island – Ap Lei Chau – and city areas are often thronged with crowds, it takes very little time to find relative tranquillity. Hills appear as if by magic amid the urban sprawl, and trails lead up them towards spectacular views. To discover Hong Kong's lower-rise lush rural pockets, hop on a slick Mass Transit Railway (MTR) train to the New Territories, or take a short ferry ride to one of the sparsely populated outlying islands.

Back in the city, the famous skyline is best enjoyed at twilight, either from the waterfront promenade at the tip of Kowloon, aboard a harbour evening cruise, or from above at The Peak on Hong Kong Island. A nightly light-and-laser display incorporating some of the most prominent, outlandish skyscrapers gives the city a surreal edge.

Street signs are in English and Chinese, English is widely understood in the main neighbourhoods, and Hong Kong is one of the world's safest cities – so enjoy.

in the mood for...

.... architecture

Hong Kong is perceived as one continuous skyscraper zone – and this is correct in most urban areas. In recent years, height restrictions in Kowloon have been lifted and some very flamboyant structures went up – the **ICC Tower** *(p.105)* has become the territory's tallest building, soaring almost half a kilometre into the sky. Truly remarkable modern landmarks include Sir Norman Foster's **HSBC Headquarters**, which appears as if its structural rigging is inside out, and the equally spectacular **Bank of China Tower** by I.M. Pei *(pp.26–7)*.

The few remnants of historic architecture are not so much stunning as evocative of eras past. Both hailing from the early 20th century and worth a look are the stately **LegCo Building** *(p.26)*, used for daily government debate, and the **Old Wan Chai Post Office** *(p.80)*. Though built in the last century, the beautifully embellished **Chi Lin Nunnery** *(p.100)* is a fine example of traditional Chinese architecture, modelled on the classic style of the Tang Dynasty.

.... no-nonsense Cantonese fare

Rice is unquestionably the staple of Cantonese cuisine, but dining gets no earthier than a bowl of steaming noodle soup. Noodle shops dot almost every main thoroughfare and small street. Outside Central's interconnecting world of indoor malls, basic noodle shops are sprinkled along Wellington Street and seem never to close; along this strip. The best quality bowl is topped with fresh house roasted duck or goose at **Yung Kee** (*p.58*).

For rice with robustly flavoured steamed seafood, braised meat and fresh vegetables, head for the animated dining room at **Lin Heung** in Sheung Wan (*p.58*). Dim sum can be another no-nonsense Cantonese dining experience, from breakfast time till early afternoon. Select a few bamboo baskets of dumplings, deep-fried spring rolls and desserts at **City Hall Maxim's Palace** (*p.33*); arrive early to grab a numbered ticket, as no pre-bookings are taken. Or try the esteemed roast pigeon served in simple outdoor restaurants in **Fo Tan** in the New Territories (*p.126*).

.... fine dining

If Hong Kong does earthy Cantonese food well, its top-tier restaurants are even more critically well received, especially internationally – both Zagat and Michelin food guides started putting out local editions in the late noughties.

The jewel in the culinary crown belongs to elegant **Lung King Heen** (*p.33*), whose light dim sum sometimes get the surprise addition of a prized Western ingredient. Also top-notch is longer-established **Shang Palace** (*p.92*), where you'll enjoy outstanding food and service under its red ceiling lanterns.

Bridging the gap between Eastern and Western fine cuisine is **Bo Innovation** (*p.37*), where the chef's classical French training is applied to deconstructed and re-interpreted Cantonese traditions – with exciting results. No such experimentation at **L'Atelier de Joël Robuchon** (*p.37*), where the creations of France's culinary king provide the expected taste-bud wow factor.

Back to the finer side of fusion, with another international celebrity chef: **Nobu** (*p.101*). The familiar yet memorable Japanese-meets-South American menu with Western sensibilities is served in an elegant dining room.

.... a night on the town

Once upon a time, visitors to Hong Kong craving a big night out had only the hotel bar or the expat hang-out Lan Kwai Fong to choose between. That's not to say that **Lan Kwai Fong** (*p.38*) isn't still a decent night out: the area has a large Chuppie (Chinese yuppie) presence, and it's popular with the partying executive set too.

These days, though, good-timers can take their pick of lively nightspots. Raise the bling factor further just around the corner in **Soho** (*p.54*); bars here are often more intimate, and its velvet-roped venues like **Dragon-i** and **M1nt** (*p.51*) are among the hottest nightspots in town.

Raucous, expensive but really buzzing are the banker-crowd bars on the fourth-floor roof podium at the **Two IFC** tower; a slightly quieter alternative is **Blue Bar** (*p.29*). Tsim Sha Tsui is home to the happening haunts of **Knutsford Terrace** and vibrant Philippe Starck-designed **Felix** (*p.96*), which also has a great view.

Speaking of views, loftily perched **Aqua Spirit** (*p.104*) offers a panoramic backdrop and theatrical lighting for a Hong Kong cocktail to remember.

.... a quiet escape in the city

As almost no one in Hong Kong has a garden, the city's handful of urban parks are very well used. The clever landscaping of **Hong Kong Park** *(pictured; p.30)* somehow means it never feels crowded. Relax with a book on one of the benches around the lake, take a break in the café and a stroll through the aviary. Or walk the lush **Wan Chai Green Trail** *(p.80)* and within minutes you will find yourself high above Hong Kong Island's bustling streets.

Provided it's not a lunar festival day, larger temples can be sanctuaries: **Tai Sin** and **Chi Lin Nunnery** *(p.100)* in Kowloon both have beautifully landscaped gardens and the temple buildings themselves are very easy on the eye. If it's a weekday, catch a taxi or board a bus to the beaches at **Shek O** *(p.148)* or **Stanley** *(p.146)*, which only get busy at weekends and public and school holidays.

.... getting sporty

Hong Kong is surrounded by the South China Sea, and the weather is warm for most of the year, so water sports are an enjoyable pastime here. Give windsurfing a go on **Cheung Chau Island** (p.160), or enjoy water-ski and wakeboard sessions on the **Southside** of Hong Kong Island (p.140). Over in the **New Territories**, ride an ex-racehorse or kayak around the mangrove-lined coastline (p.132), or rent a bike and explore stunning **Plover Cove Country Park** (p.123).

.... a lazy day

Soho's laid-back cafés (p.50) are perfect for whiling away the morning hours. You could then stroll down **Hollywood Road**, popping into antique shops (p.53) and art galleries (p.52) that catch your eye. Then board a Hong Kong Island tram and let the driver do all the work; whether you head east or west, sit back and take it all in (p.39). Follow that with a snaking taxi ride up to **The Peak** (p.42). Stroll the one-hour flat circular route with its great Hong Kong vistas, or if that's too much effort, grab a drink or meal in a restaurant with views (p.41).

GIORGIO ARMANI

.... retail therapy

No visit to Hong Kong is complete without visiting a mall or three. In fact, city development in the past two decades has made it almost impossible to avoid doing so, as they're often pedestrian thoroughfares.

For those looking to buy top-tier designer brands, **Central** *(p.28)* and **Causeway Bay** *(p.82)* are home to the glitziest malls on Hong Kong Island, with some top European and US fashions, watches and jewellery specifically designed for the Asian market. The

Island Beverly in Causeway Bay *(p.82)* and Tsim Sha Tsui's **Rise Commercial Centre** *(p.106)* have cutting-edge clothes and accessories from local and Japanese and Korean designers.

Find clothing bargains in over-run shops in Wan Chai's **Johnston Road** *(p.77)*, Central's **Pedder Building** *(p.34)*, and at **Stanley Market** *(p.146)*, which is also a good souvenir-hunting ground. Best quality Mainland China products, though, come from specialist department stores *(p.103)*.

.... a proper escape in a far-flung corner

You don't have to be a hiker to head up to the **New Territories**. Leave the high-rises behind and aim for **Sai Kung** *(p.121)* to see why some Hong Kongers choose to live out in parts that are not dependent on MTR train connections. Mountains, colourful plant nurseries and a village with plenty of cafés, bars and seafront restaurants await. If you want to exercise your leg muscles once you get there, head into nearby inland or coastal country parks for a hike or a snorkel *(p.119)*. Nearby, **Clearwater Bay**'s fine sand beaches *(p.118)*, with showers, lifeguards and food kiosks, are very quiet on weekdays.

For a breath of fresh air in what can sometimes be a stifling city, jump on a ferry to one of Hong Kong's outlying islands and watch the city disappear in your wake. The most low-key of all the islands are **Grass Island** *(p.135)* and **Peng Chau** *(p.162)*. Or charter a junk or pleasure boat *(p.166)* and drop anchor wherever you fancy.

.... being entertained

Hong Kong Arts Centre and **Hong Kong Academy for Performing Arts** are among the most accessible theatres, putting on the biggest-budget theatre, music and dance performances from local orchestras and production companies *(p.78)*. Less mainstream performances are held at the independent **Fringe Club** *(p.56)* and smaller government theatres across Hong Kong. For a laugh, check out **TakeOut Comedy** or listen to jazz at **Peel Fresco** *(both p.56)*.

.... the full-on city buzz

The pace of life in Hong Kong is dynamic. Office workers stride with purpose while talking business on smart phones; shoppers in swanky areas are loaded up with designer bags. Nowhere will you feel this urban heartbeat more than on the main roads of **Causeway Bay** *(p.82)*, **Tsim Sha Tsui** *(pp.93, 98, 106, 107 and 110)* and **Mong Kok** *(pp.97 and 109)*, where glitzy shops alternate with juice vendors and key-cutters. In **Central** *(pp.26–7 and 34)*, it's an upmarket experience – and the buzz is at its peak during lunch hours and early evening.

.... local culture

A few museums give a great background on Hong Kong's cultural origins: notably, the **Heritage Museum** *(pictured; also p.122)*, which spotlights the Southern Chinese ethnic groups that have made Hong Kong home, as well as indigenous beliefs and practices. Get a feel for how much less westernised Hong Kong once was – from its development as a Treaty Port up to the pre-skyscraper first half of the 20th century – by perusing the photos, illustrations and paintings in the **Museum of History** and **Museum of Art** *(p.95)*.

To witness modern-day culture in action, take a walk around the periphery of **Temple Street Market** *(p.97)*: fortune tellers give alfresco palm and face readings, restaurant tables are set up outdoors, and elderly musicians play folk and operatic music on the pavement.

Take part in two current social passions with a dim sum lunch *(p.33)* on a Sunday at elegant **Lung King Heen** or buzzing **City Hall Maxim's Palace**; or cheer on your horse on a Wednesday night at **Happy Valley Racecourse** *(p.85)*.

.... being pampered

Spas in Hong Kong's top hotels are ranked among the world's best, and the city is something of a leader in fusing Eastern and Western manipulation techniques and treatment ingredients. Spas at the Hong Kong-based Mandarin Oriental Group have made a point of this with their own house oils and creams – try them at the cosy **Landmark Mandarin Oriental** *(p.44)*. **Spa at Four Seasons** *(p.44)* is possibly Hong Kong's roomiest, with sprawling spaces that house large bubbling vitality pools, steam and shower rooms. The **Peninsula Spa** *(p.44)* has very luxurious suites with great Hong Kong Island views. And relative newcomer **Mira Spa** *(p.32)* offers both quality treatments and a refreshingly bright interior and staff demeanour.

Many of these places offer massages and facials targeted at men, but amid all the top-end female-oriented beauty salons in town the ultimate destination for guys who like grooming is the Art Deco-inspired **Mandarin Barber** *(p.32)*.

.... family fun

Add an element of excitement to your sightseeing by choosing a fun form of transport. Ride a clunking vintage tram (*p.66*); or get hauled up Hong Kong Island's most famous mountain at a weird angle on a funicular railway (*p.39*) – with **Madame Tussaud's** waiting at the top; or ride the world's longest series of covered escalators (*p.65*). Kids will also love the **Ngong Ping 360** (*p.155*), a long cable-car ride above a lush Lantau Island mountain, overlooking islets that dot the South China Sea and aircraft coming and going from the airport.

Hong Kong Disneyland (*p.158*) is always a winner with kids, and families can enjoy marine life and mammals as well as rides at enduring family favourite **Ocean Park** (*p.149*). There's more educational fun at the interactive **Science** and **Space Museums** (*p.95*) and the **Railway Museum** (*p.122*).

Finally, a trip to Aberdeen's floating **Jumbo Kingdom** restaurant always seems to go down well with the wee set (*p.143*).

neighbourhoods

Some of Hong Kong Island's swankiest office, shopping and residential areas are found in Central, Admiralty and Mid-Levels, though re-developing Kowloon is fast catching up. The bars and restaurants of Soho and Noho merge into Hong Kong's antique and art gallery area, and westward into earthy Sheung Wan. To the east, Wan Chai and Causeway Bay offer an authentic taste of modern Hong Kong, with some great shopping and nightlife. Just outside all this bustle are the hilly New Territories and outlying islands.

Central, Mid-Levels, Admiralty and The Peak From the gleaming malls and towers around Exchange Square in Central, which are home to some of the best restaurants in Asia, Hong Kong Island rises through the exclusive residential towers of Mid-Levels up to The Peak. Hong Kong Park and places of worship offer relatively quiet sanctuaries and the Peak Tram whisks you up to the most spacious green enclave of this neighbourhood.

Soho, Noho, Sheung Wan and Western Soho and Noho, which are abbreviations of South and North of Hollywood Road, sprang up after the world's longest covered series of escalators was built in the early 1990s. Their international cafés, bars, restaurants, small performance venues, and boutiques offer cosy and sometimes offbeat diversions. Sheung Wan and Western offer a grittier, more traditional Hong Kong vista of dried foods and herbal medicine merchants.

Wan Chai, Causeway Bay and Happy Valley Restaurants and bars in Wan Chai and Causeway Bay offer some of the territory's best selection of down-to-earth eating and drinking, though there are some highbrow and high-floor exceptions with panoramic harbour backdrops. Causeway Bay has traditional department stores alongside hipster boutiques. A visit to Happy Valley Racetrack is a great, energising people-watching experience.

Kowloon Once the earthier side of the harbour, the peninsula of Kowloon still has plenty of no-nonsense neighbourhoods, but its southern tip has some very 21st-century pockets. It's the place to come for markets, museums and magnificent views. A little further northeast are the landscaped grounds of Wong Tai Sin Temple, the most colourful place of worship in Hong Kong, and tranquil Chi Lin Nunnery.

New Territories The land between Kowloon and mainland China makes up the New Territories – so called as it was ceded to the colonial British government later than Hong Kong Island and Kowloon. Pre-1970s it was mostly arable and livestock farmland; after that, new towns were built to house the growing population. It's still home to villages, country parks, great beaches and spacious temple complexes.

Southside In contrast to the northern coast of Hong Kong Island, the rocky southern shore remains relatively unspoilt. Stanley has a decent beach on one bay, with restaurants and bars lining another, plus the Maritime Museum and a souvenir and clothing market. The rides and dolphins at Ocean Park remain a major draw and Aberdeen Harbour is immediately recognisable for its flotilla of bobbing junks and sampans housing what remains of Hong Kong's 'boat people'.

Lantau and Outer Islands A quick ferry ride from the edge of Central lies a low-rise, low-population side to Hong Kong that many visitors don't see. Laid-back waterfront restaurants and a smattering of bars are found on Cheung Chau, Lantau, Lamma and Peng Chau Islands. All offer scenic hikes and good beaches. Lantau's cable car connects with the world's largest outdoor seated bronze Buddha; plus Hong Kong Disneyland is here.

Huangbejing
Sha Tau Kok
Sha Tau Kok Hoi
Kat O Chau
(Crooked Island)
Tsing Chau Lek
Ngo Mei Chau
(Crescent Island)
Tai Pang Wan
(Mirs Bay)
Nam Chung
Luk Keng
Wong Wan Chau
(Double Island)
Tiu Tang Lung
▲ 416
Wu Kau Tang
Wong Chuk Kok Hoi
Bluff
Head
Fanling
439
Cloudy Hill
639
Wong Leng
Chek Chau
(Port Island)
Tai Chek Mun
(North Channel)
Flat Island
Ocean
Point
Tap Mun Chau
(Grass Island)
Plover Cove
Reservoir
Chek Mun Hoi Hap
(Tolo Channel)
Jone's
Cove
Pak
Sha O
Shuen
Wan
Tai Po
Yim Tin
Tsai
Tolo Harbour
Ma Shi
Chau
Pak Sha Tau Chau
(Harbour Island)
Sham Chung
▲ 468
Sharp Peak
Tsuen Valley
Taj Po Kau
Wu Kai
Sha
Shap
Heung
▲ 481
Shek Uk Shan
Mo Shan
Ma
Liu Shui
Ma On Shan
Tai Shui
Hang
Ma On Shan
▲ 702
*Tai Long
Wan*
Tai Chau
r r i t o r i e s
Temple of
10,000 Buddhas
Penfold Park
Racetrack
Yim Tin
Tsai
Sai Kung
Tai Tau
Chau
High Island Reservoir
Sha Tin
HK Heritage
Museum
*Sai
Kung
Hoi*
Kiu Tsui
Chau
Leung Shuen Wan Chau
(High Island)
*heung
ai Chung*
Beacon Hill
452
Kowloon
Peak
602
Kau Sai
Chau
Fu Tau Fan Chau
(Town Island)
*Kwai
ung*
Cheung Sha Wan
San Po
Kong
*Ngau Mei Hoi
(Port Shelter)*
Tiu
Chung
Chau
Wang Chau
*hi Wan
Sham Shui Po*
Mong Kok
KOWLOON
Hung
Hom
Kwun Tong
Tseung
Kwan O
Shelter
Island
Ung Kong
(Bluff Island)
Fo Shek Chau
(Basalt Island)
Hang
Hau
Tsim Sha Tsui
Tiu Keng
Leng
Clear
Water
Bay
Country
Park
Trio Island
*eung
Wan*
*Victoria
Harbour*
North
Point
Yau Tong
Lung Ha Wan
Central
Causeway
Bay
Tsak Yue Chung
(Quarry Bay)
Tseung
Kwan O
(Junk Bay)
Clearwater Bay
Ching Chau
(Steep Island)
Kwo Chau Kwan To
(Ninepin Group)
Wan Chai
Tai Hang
Shau
Kei Wan
Joss
House
Bay
Pak Kwo
Chau
*Victoria
Peak*
Hong Kong Island
Chai Wan
Cape
Collinson
Fat Tong Mun
Nam Kwo
Chau
Lam
Aberdeen
Wong Chuk
Hang
Shek O
Tung Lung
Chau
Tathong
Point
S O U T H
*Pok Liu Hoi Hap
(Lamma Channel)*
Ocean
Park
Middle
Island
Stanley
*Tai Tam
Wan*
D'Aguilar
Peninsula
Cape d'Aguilar
C H I N A
Tung O Wan
Round
Island
**Stanley
Peninsula**
Sheung Mun
Po Toi Islands
Waglan
Island
S E A
*Yuen
Kok*
Bluff Head
Beaufort
Island
Sung Kong
*nt
house*
ai Kok
Po Toi

21

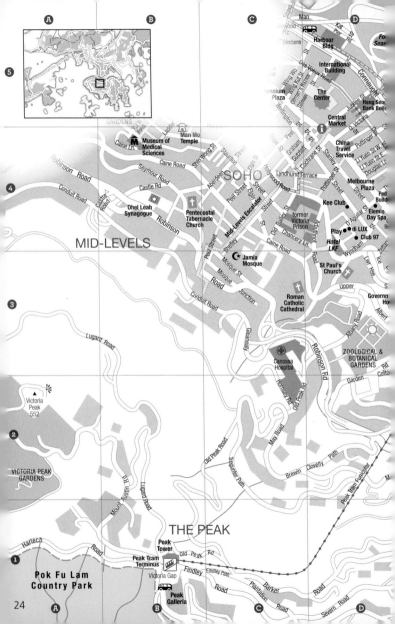

Ⓐ   Ⓑ   Ⓒ   Ⓓ

Ⓔ

GARDENS

Museum of Medical Sciences

Man Mo Temple

Caine Ln.

Caine Road

Shin Wong St

Staunton

Elgin St

Graham

Gutzlaff

Cochrane St

Stanley St

SOHO

Robinson   Road

Seymour Road

Castle Rd

Aberdeen

Peel Street

Hollywood Road

Lyndhurst Terrace

Pottinger

Man Wo

Bird St

Sincere

Harbour Bldg

Kat Pier Rd

International Building

Fo Seas

Connaught

Millennium Plaza

The Center

Central Market

Jubilee St

Queen

Des Vieux Road

Wing Wo

Wing Kut St

Gilman Bazaar

Wellington

China Travel Service

Hang Seng Bank Buildi

Victoria St

Pottinger St

Li Yuen St W.

Li Yuen St E.

Douglas Lr

Melbourne Plaza

D'Aguilar St

Kee Club

Elemis Day Spa

Play

di LUX

Club 97

Hotel LKF

Wyndham

Ped Build

Robinson   Road

Conduit Road

Ohel Leah Synagogue

Castle Road

Pentecostal Tabernacle Church

Mid-Levels Escalator

Former Victoria Prison

Chancery Ln.

Caine Road

MID-LEVELS

Peel Street

Shelley

Elgin

Staunton

Ladder

Robinson

Jamia Mosque

Mosque St

Mosque   Road

Junction

Conduit Road

Roman Catholic Cathedral

St Paul's Church

Upper

Govern Ho

Albert

Lugard Road

Canossa Hospital

Glenealy

Robinson Rd

Old Peak Rd

ZOOLOGICAL & BOTANICAL GARDENS

Garden

Cotto

▲ **Victoria Peak 552**

Ramsey Rd

May Road

VICTORIA PEAK GARDENS

Old Peak Road

Tregunter Path

Mount Austin

PH.

Lugard Road

Brewin

Clovelly   Path

Peak Tram Funicular

M

THE PEAK

Harlech

Road

Pok Fu Lam Country Park

Peak Tower

Peak Tram Terminus

Victoria Gap

Old Peak Rd

Findley

Findley Path

Peak Galleria

Findley   Road

Barker

Plantation

Road

Severn   Road

Road

Ⓐ   Ⓑ   Ⓒ   Ⓓ

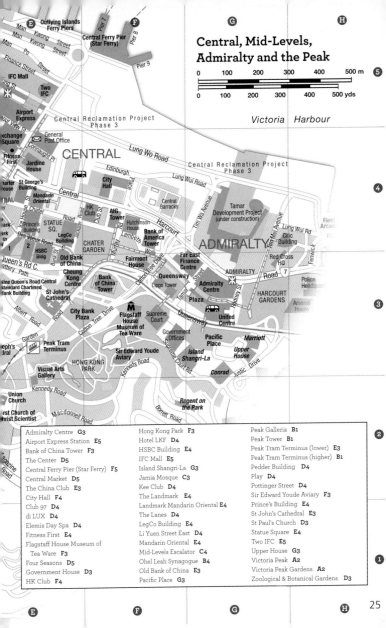

Central, Mid-Levels, Admiralty and the Peak

| 0 | 100 | 200 | 300 | 400 | 500 m |
| 0 | 100 | 200 | 300 | 400 | 500 yds |

Victoria Harbour

Central Reclamation Project Phase 3

Central Reclamation Project Phase 3

CENTRAL

ADMIRALTY

Tamar Development Project (under construction)

Contrast three grand **colonial structures** with some snazzy **skyscrapers**

Three of Hong Kong's finest remaining colonial buildings are found in Central district. This traditionally administrative area has also always been Hong Kong's financial hub and premier office address and, as such, it is home to many of the territory's most imposing high-rise towers.

From the 1950s, impressive colonnaded buildings gave way to taller buildings, maximising the same plots of land. That few remain is indicative of Hong Kong's long-standing indifference to heritage preservation.

Thankfully, in the last few years public pressure has forced a closer look at buildings that had been earmarked for possible redevelopment. One of the most precious remaining heritage structures is the government **LegCo Building** (*pictured*; 8 Jackson Road; tel: 2869 9200; www.legco.gov.hk; map E4) next to Chater Gardens. It opened its stately doors in 1912, when it began life as the Supreme Court Building. Although it has been home to Hong Kong's Legislative Council since 1985, a statue of Themis, the Greek goddess of divine law and order, still stands guard outside its main entrance. Unless you have good reason to request in advance

a visit inside, study its arcaded stone exterior with its Greek, European and Chinese features.

Nearby, the **Old Bank of China Building** (2A Des Voeux Road Central; map E3) qualified as a skyscraper when built in 1950, but its 17 storeys put it in the shadow of many buildings today. Its style combines late Art Deco and Communist Modernism. Nowadays it houses the China Club (*p.45*) and financial offices.

Uphill just above Central is **Government House** (Upper Albert Road; tel: 2508 1234; www.ceo.gov.hk/gh; map D3). As the residence of Hong Kong's Chief Executive, it is only open to the public one weekend per year but its facade can be seen through the gateposts. Twenty-five British colonial governors lived here: Sir John Bowring was the first, in October 1855, and Chris Patten the last.

In contrast to these heritage landmarks is one of Central's iconic modern towers: I.M. Pei's stunning **Bank of China Tower** (*pictured*; 1 Garden Road; tel: 2826 6888; www.bochk.com; Mon–Fri 9am–6pm, Sat 9am–1pm; map F3). At 70 storeys and 369 metres tall, its zigzagging form made it Asia's tallest building when it opened in 1990. At the time it was thought that its sharp angles radiated poor feng shui, but that controversy was short-lived. There is a small 43rd-floor viewing deck.

A few minutes away is **HSBC Headquarters** (1 Queen's Road; tel: 2822 1111; map E4), a multi-layered glass and metal construction designed by Sir Norman Foster and completed in 1985. At its elevated base are two large bronze lions, originally on guard duty at the bank's former 1935 incarnation.

Rising highest in Central, next to the Hong Kong Stock Exchange, is **Two IFC**, commonly referred to as IFC (International Finance Centre; 8 Finance Street; www.ifc.com. hk; map E5). Completed in 2003, the building is notable for its 88 storeys – though there is no public viewing floor.

A little west from here, **The Center** (99 Queen's Road; map D5) is visible from all directions at night, as its 73 storeys are clad with decorative lighting panels that emit vivid rainbow shades.

Observe *tai-tais* – ladies who **lunch and shop** – in their natural habitat

Financial crises may come and go, but Hong Kong's high-end *tai-tais* didn't miss a beat. *Tai-tai* literally means wife in Cantonese. But the label is also attached to the top-tier lady of leisure in Hong Kong, who more often than not is married to a wealthy husband.

You can observe the fashionable ladies who lunch, and join them for high tea, wherever top designer labels are sold in Central, particularly at the swish shops of **The Landmark** and **Prince's Building**, and at the more exclusive upper-floor boutiques of **IFC Mall**.

Hong Kong's branch of UK department store **Harvey Nichols** in The Landmark has the double *tai-tai* temptation of top international labels and its **Fourth Floor** restaurant and bar (tel: 3695 3389), a great, discreet lunch and tea spot. IFC's **Isola** restaurant (*pictured*) is a handy upscale pit

stop on the same level as one of Hong Kong's most opulent malls, **Lane Crawford** (tel: 2118 3388; www.lanecrawford.com). And Prince's Building's sprawling restaurant **Sevva** (25/F; tel: 2537 1388; www.sevva.hk), with its wraparound sofa-strewn wooden-decked terrace, fine pastries and cocktail bar, is owned by one of the glitterati set.

Another favourite *tai-tai* haunt is the **Mandarin Oriental**'s low-lit **Clipper Lounge**, a long-standing refreshment and chat spot.

The Landmark; 16 Des Voeux Road Central; map E4
Prince's Building; 10 Chater Road; map E4
IFC Mall; 8 Finance Street; map E5
Clipper Lounge; Mandarin Oriental Hong Kong, 5 Connaught Road; tel: 2825 4007; www.mandarinoriental.com; map E4

Drink in the deal-making buzz with Hong Kong's **movers and shakers**

Hong Kong's banking district is home to some lively watering holes. A clutch of bars near Exchange Square, with great drinks and harbour views, is abuzz with an international mix of bankers on weekdays from 5–7pm, once local trading has ended.

G Bar, atop Two IFC's rooftop podium, is a cracker. Basically a high-ceilinged glass-walled box, it has panoramic views across Victoria Harbour and back, across IFC's elevated garden and into the towers of Central. Grab a stool at a tall table or sit at the long bar where cocktails are exuberantly shaken. Martinis with fresh fruit and champagne mixes are popular; top-tier bar food includes mini burgers with thick-cut fries, and a cured ham and parmesan salad. Music cranks up from early evening; outdoor lounge seating is more chilled, but it's still a dynamic Hong Kong atmosphere.

On the same rooftop level, **Red Bar** and **Isola** also offer killer cocktails and premium wine and snack lists; Red has a healthier menu and Isola is Italian-inspired.

Nearby, **Blue Bar** at the **Four Seasons** attracts a similar crowd but is cosier and lower key than the IFC bars. Bag a low-slung armchair or sofa at a window table for a harbour vista. Besides its 88 blue-coloured cocktails, plenty of other concoctions plus wine and beer are offered. There is a complementary snack buffet daily from 5.30–7.30pm and a jazz band plays from Thursday to Saturday.

G Bar; tel: 2805 0629; www.jcgroup. hk; Red Bar; tel: 8129 8882; www.pure-red.com; Isola; tel: 2383 8765; www. isolabarandgrill.com; all 4/F, Two IFC, 8 Finance Street; map E5
Blue Bar; Four Seasons Hotel Hong Kong; 8 Finance Street; tel: 3196 8830; www.fourseasons.com; map D5

Get an eyeful of greenery at **Hong Kong Park**

The fenced-in quiet grounds of **Hong Kong Park** are situated a little uphill from most of the Central bustle, and are a calm spot from which to take in the surrounding towering cityscape.

Though it only opened in 1991, the planting of mature trees makes this welcome green space seem as though it's been here for decades. Stretching 8 hectares, from above the Lan Kwai Fong party zone in Central to Admiralty, this well-landscaped

haven has a waterfall and stream, a central duck pond and benches everywhere – so take a load off your feet and relax.

The fountain near the Admiralty end is crossed by a walkway, allowing for the popular photo opportunity of seemingly walking through it – be aware that you may get a bit wet from the spray. Nearby is restaurant and bar **L16**; its sunken open-sided light wood interior and outdoor garden tables are an excellent quiet spot for a cocktail, meal or cup of tea. If you want to know more about the latter, the **Flagstaff House Museum of Tea Ware** is in the grounds (*opposite*).

Hong Kong Park; main entrance at 16 Cotton Tree Drive; www.lcsd.gov.hk/ parks; daily 6am–11pm; free; map F3
L16; tel: 2522 6333; map F3

PARK AVIARY
The **Sir Edward Youde Aviary** (*pictured*) is a highlight of the park. Named after the late Governor of Hong Kong (from 1982 to 1986), its ample netted space gives you the chance to see a rare commodity in Hong Kong – wildlife. Information boards describe the habits of some 100 species of local and regional birds who live in this simulated sub-tropical forest.

Take tea very seriously at the **Flagstaff House Museum of Tea Ware**

In a quiet nook of Hong Kong Park, towards the Admiralty gate end, the **Flagstaff House Museum of Tea Ware** is a curious find. The structure itself is a rarity – the oldest surviving colonial building in the city, built around 1845, served as the official residence of the Commander of British Forces until 1978. Its whitewashed two storeys with colonnaded porches, against a wall of lush greenery, make it popular with newlyweds as a photo backdrop (there is a marriage registry office within the park).

The permanent collection describes the cultivation of tea, the different brews, how it is processed (immediately dried or fermented first) and the rituals that surround serving it – both in China and beyond.

Frequently changing exhibitions showcase tea-related paraphernalia, from beautifully glazed cups and pots from around the world to drawings and paintings on the subject. Cultivation,

serving procedure and a history of teatime implements are all covered. The late collector K.S. Lo donated a collection of prized Yixing teapots in his will in 1995. These fine ceramic pieces are displayed in their own gallery. Alongside exhibitions, the museum holds regular tea gatherings and lectures to promote Chinese ceramic art and tea-drinking culture in tandem.

In the gift shop you get the chance to buy some of the best-quality pots and tea types you might find in Hong Kong.

Flagstaff House Museum of Tea Ware; 10 Cotton Tree Drive; tel: 2869 0690; www.lcsd.gov.hk; Wed–Mon 10am–5pm, closed public holidays; free; map F3

Freshen up, gentlemen, with a visit to a **traditional barber** or **modern salon**

If you're hankering for some pampering, then you won't have to look far in the Central district – choose between a traditional barber shop or a tranquil spa for a break from the city buzz.

For an old-school wet shave or trim, there is none better than the **Mandarin Barber** shop (*pictured*; Mandarin Oriental Hong Kong, 5 Connaught Road; tel: 2825 4088; www.mandarinoriental.com; map E4). Some of its practitioners have been expertly wielding the soap brush, cut-throat razor, clippers and scissors for decades. In the Art Deco-style waiting area the visitor is offered tea or coffee while sitting in a leather armchair. Vintage barber chairs and hot towels await.

Metrosexual gents may prefer a facial at **Elemis Day Spa** (9/F,

Century Square, 1 D'Aguilar Street; tel: 2521 6660; www.elemisdayspa.com.hk; map D4), a small-scale Zen-inspired downtown salon. It offers three varieties, including the Cooling Hot Stone Body-Facial, which incorporates body massage using extremes of temperature.

Over in Kowloon, notable men's spa treatments include the Tao of Detox package at **Chuan Spa** at **Langham Place** hotel (555 Shanghai Street, Mong Kok; tel: 3552 3510; www.chuanspa.com; map p.90 B7): a de-stressing scrub, massage and facial. Bright, down-to-earth **Mira Spa** at **The Mira** hotel (118 Nathan Road, Tsim Sha Tsui; tel: 2315 5500; www.themirahotel.com; map p.90 C2) offers the Mira Man facial and a deep Muscle Melt massage.

Be seated for a **dim sum** experience to remember

A speciality of Cantonese cuisine is dim sum. Small, mostly savoury, dishes – steamed, deep-fried or braised – are eaten for breakfast, brunch or lunch, and usually enjoyed with a pot of tea that is endlessly topped up.

Though the occasional chef has developed creative dim sum adaptations, a core of favourite items tends to remain the same. In some restaurants, such as the buzzing **City Hall Maxim's Palace**, dishes are wheeled around on heated trolleys. Trolley labels are solely in Chinese characters, but

feel free to lift lids and see what's inside – or consult the bilingual menu at the table. This popular restaurant cannot be booked, so arrive before you feel very hungry, take a numbered ticket and wait your turn. The food, atmosphere and harbour view are worth it.

Also along the waterfront, elegant **Lung King Heen** at the **Four Seasons Hotel Hong Kong** presents a dim sum menu list that includes refined takes on classics – the *siu mai* combines chopped premium pork, rather than mince, with large crunchy shrimps; there are steamed lobster and scallop dumplings; or baked puffs of whole abalone and diced chicken.

Edgy-looking **Zen**, in Admiralty, actually serves up a pretty traditional menu: dim sum-sized house specials include deep-fried chicken wing stuffed with sticky rice and dried shrimp, and a few varieties of filled, steamed rice-flour rolls.

City Hall Maxim's Palace; 2/F, Low Block, City Hall, 7 Edinburgh Place; tel: 2521 1303; map F4
Lung King Heen; 4/F, Four Seasons Hotel Hong Kong, 8 Finance Street; tel: 3196 8880; map D5
Zen; lower G/F, 1 Pacific Place, 88 Queensway; tel: 2845 4555; map G3

Climb **The Pedder Building** and amble through **'The Lanes'** for clothing bargains

With its anonymous entrance and lift lobby, tucked between the Shanghai Tang store on its ground floor and the busy, highly illuminated HSBC, the **Pedder Building** in the heart of throbbing Central could easily be missed. But seek it out for its shops selling discounted clothes and toys, plus its atmospheric, retro Art Deco teahouse, the **China Tee Club** (1/F; tel: 2521 0233).

For a thorough look, take a lift up to the top of this 1920s building and then use the staircase down to peruse its low-price stores. Some branded items from previous seasons can usually be found, plus plenty of quality wool, cashmere and silk garments. **3rd Avenue** (Shop 304B, 3/F) stocks vintage leather products, including top designer handbags.

More casual brand-name over-runs can be found along the narrow pedestrian-only streets nicknamed **'The Lanes'**. Formally called Li Yuen Street East and Li Yuen Street West, linking Des Voeux Road and Queen's Road in Central, here you can find bargain clothing (especially for women and children), handbags, accessories and shoes, alongside haberdashery products.

A little further west along Queen's Road, **Pottinger Street** is also worth a rummage. As this cobbled street climbs upward towards Lyndhurst Terrace in Soho, shops line both sides and their vivid wares spill out onto the street, on rails and in boxes. Party costumes are what first catch the eye – this is the place to come to transform yourself into a Chinese empress or Spiderman.

Pedder Building; 12 Pedder Street; map D4
The Lanes; Li Yuen Street East and Li Yuen Street West; map D4

Drink in the views with a **classy cocktail** at the **Café Gray Deluxe** bar

Perched on the 49th floor of boutique hotel The Upper House, atop Pacific Place Mall in Admiralty, is one of the latest favourites of the well-heeled: the **Café Gray Deluxe** bar.

The bar is named after chef Gray Kunz – who was highly regarded in Hong Kong over two decades ago, made it big in the US with Michelin-starred Café Gray, and is now back within these modern luxe walls. The narrow bar joins, but is not fully visible to, a modern fine-dining restaurant. A plate-glass window lined with booths faces the bar counter, and views stretch past the tops of Admiralty's towers, across Victoria harbour to Tsim Sha Tsui.

Knowledgeable bar staff serve up lesser-known wine varieties, all simply explained upon request and with plenty available by the glass. There are more familiar choices, too, plus a tempting bar snacks menu.

For a lower-key drink and bar snack but of a similarly high standard, head for the little-known unnamed bar on the 8th floor of the **Conrad Hong Kong** hotel, which resides between two restaurants (Brasserie on the Eighth and Nicholini's). Enjoy particularly fine wines, with a large European selection, or plenty of other refined beverages, with a city view and top service in quiet lounge-bar surrounds.

Café Gray Deluxe bar; 49/F, The Upper House, Pacific Place, 88 Queensway; tel: 2918 1838; www.cafegrayhk.com; map G3 Bar on the 8th floor of Conrad Hong Kong, Pacific Place; 88 Queensway; tel: 2521 3838; map G3

Grab a **top-deck tram or bus seat** and take in the sights, sounds and smells of the **north shore streets**

A trip on a vintage tram as it trundles slowly across the north shore of Hong Kong Island through animated streets, is a great way to feel the pulse of the city – as well as the quickest method of travelling short distances. The tram has changed little since the first generation were launched in 1904. At that time, they were single-decked; the design of the double-decker

version used today dates from 1925. Thanks to their windows usually being open, you can see, hear and smell the environment as you roll through it. From Central, head to the Western district past dried seafood and medicinal herb shops; or head east past the LegCo Building and Norman Foster's HSBC Building (p.27) to weave through Wan Chai's earthy bustle and Causeway Bay's frenetic shopping streets (p.82). Pay the flat two-dollar fare as you get off.

Open-topped buses are a newer way to soak up the city. From Central's Star Ferry stop (map F5), **Big Bus Tours** loops around Central, Soho and along the Wan Chai waterfront, or heads to the scenic southside. Also picked up at a Star Ferry bus stop, **Rickshaw Sightseeing Bus** offers one route west to Pok Fu Lam via Hollywood Road and Sheung Wan, and another east to Happy Valley via Wan Chai and Causeway Bay. Hop on and off at any point with a day pass.

Hong Kong Tramways; tel: 2548 7102; www.hktramways.com
Big Bus Tours; tel: 2723 2108; www. bigbustours.com
Rickshaw Sightseeing Bus; tel: 2873 0818; www.rickshawbus.com

Become star-struck at one of two Central **French Michelin-starred outposts**

The Hong Kong dining scene has long been blessed by overseas celebrity chefs opening up outposts in the city. Two Michelin-starred French operations offer a truly world-class experience.

Don't be deceived by the informal air at **L'Atelier de Joël Robuchon**. The service here is slightly sniffy – but that can be excused when food and wine are presented at such an elevated level. Both the tasting and à la carte menus reflect what's in season in France. Expect starters such as caviar-topped crabmeat on a base of tomato jelly and avocado. Its lower-level **Salon de Thé** is a great Continental breakfast spot.

The other top French dining room on Hong Kong Island is **Pierre** at the Mandarin Oriental, which has become more approachable since superstar chef Pierre Gagnaire relaxed his

'molecular gastronomy' fixation. Gagnaire likes to take a key ingredient and serve it in a variety of unusual ways: the langoustine starter, for example, is served as tartare, in a mousse, on skewers, pan-fried and in a *velouté* sauce – and that's all one course. The dark dining room has dramatic views.

L'Atelier de Joël Robuchon; Shop 401, 4/F, The Landmark, 15 Queen's Road; tel: 2166 9000; www.joel-robuchon.com; map E4
Pierre; 25/F, Mandarin Oriental Hong Kong, 5 Connaught Road; tel: 2825 4001; www.mandarinoriental.com; map E4

BO INNOVATION

Try the creations of Hong Kong's own Michelin-starred chef Alvin Leung at **Bo Innovation** in Wan Chai (2/F, 60 Johnston Road; tel: 2850 8371; www.boinnovation. com; map p.70 C3). Trained in classic French cuisine, Leung serves up meticulously prepared tasting menus and a boundary-pushing take on Cantonese cuisine.

Party like an expat or Chuppie in **Lan Kwai Fong**

Looking at it now, it's hard to imagine that **Lan Kwai Fong**, snaking some 100 metres uphill from Central's Wellington Street, was an unremarkable street until the late 1980s. That's when the first bar with a dance floor opened. Since then, the road gradually became packed on both sides with open-fronted and basement joints, as did adjoining **D'Aguilar Street**.

Though officially different roads, the label Lan Kwai Fong now refers to both. Gradually, buildings of around eight storeys have been pulled down to make way for taller ones that house bars and restaurants. Once an expat haunt, Lan Kwai Fong now attracts mostly local party types and Chuppies (Chinese yuppies).

One nightspot that has stood the test of time is **Club 97**. The lounge bar has a clubbier feel on certain nights of the week, when it takes on music genres such as Latin and reggae.

Relative newcomer, subterranean **Play**, has high-tech lighting panels that change colour on the walls and the tiny raised dance floor. Its party piece is called Play Me – a three-glass sequential cocktail, one of which is a flaming shooter.

In the same building is a great place to enjoy a cocktail or beer, street-side **di Lux**. With its shutters rolled back you can soak up the buzz and even eat from an Italian menu: the thin-crust pizzas are good, or there are heartier mains.

Club 97; 9 Lan Kwai Fong; tel: 2810 9333; map D4
di Lux; upper G/F, California Tower, 32 D'Aguilar Street; tel: 2868 9538; www. lkfe.com; map D4
Play; basement, California Tower, 32 D'Aguilar Street; tel: 2868 6062; www. playclub.asia; map D4

Get hauled up a mountain through residential high-rises for some unusual perspectives

There is nothing quite like a ride on the **Peak Tram**. Constructed to ease the way up for privileged government officials and executive residents, the tram made its maiden trip in 1888. Formally speaking, it is a funicular railway – steel cable is attached to the cars.

From its terminus between Central and Admiralty, the ascent is immediately steep. At something like a 45-degree angle, passengers are hauled up Victoria Peak on seats facing back towards the direction they've come from. This, and the fact that the tracks cut first through the densely packed residential high-rises of the Mid-Levels district, makes for some unusual perspectives. As Victoria Harbour and Kowloon

emerge beyond, the white and pink tiled apartment towers recede to appear as spindly as toothpicks.

Then, near the end of the journey, lush palms, banyans and other vegetation obscure the view – once upon a time, most of the journey would have been like this.

For an enjoyable ride back down, take a bus from the terminus at the Peak. This is a slower, winding descent from leafy to urban through a long series of switchbacks, giving a great overview of the city. Check marked bus routes – most of Hong Kong Island is accessed.

Peak Tram; St Joseph Building, Garden Road; daily 7am–midnight; tel: 2849 7654; www.thepeak.com.hk; map E3

Feel the faith at one of **three houses of worship**

Ride up the Mid-Levels Escalator, or walk uphill from Central, to visit the temples of three faiths brought to Hong Kong from abroad. A synagogue, a mosque and a cathedral sprang up many decades ago in this affluent part of Hong Kong, where they serve as hubs of small non-indigenous religious communities. These days, plenty of Hong Kong Chinese join congregations at all three too.

In fact, marriages between local couples as well as non-Chinese are common at imposing **St John's Cathedral**. Well maintained, with whitewashed walls, vivid stained-glass windows, and built in the shape of a cross, Catholic St John's is near the Peak Tram station. Its doors are open daily to the public for quiet prayer or to attend services.

Along the Shelley Street escalator route, through swirling filigree iron gates, is **Jamia Mosque** in a small walled courtyard. Its original mid-19th-century structure, with its small minaret, was the first mosque built in Hong Kong and it was added to in 1915. Islamic visitors are permitted to attend services.

Near here is **Ohel Leah Synagogue**, built in 1902 by a banker, Sir Jacob E. Sassoon, in memory of his mother, Leah. The Eastern Jewish-style building has two storeys, to enable female worshippers to be seated in a balcony area. Its renovation in 1998 won a heritage award from Unesco. Services are held daily.

St John's Cathedral; 4-8 Garden Road; tel: 2523 4157; www.stjohnscathedral. org.hk; daily 7.30am–8pm map E3 Jamia Mosque; 30 Shelley Street; tel: 2523 7743; daily 9am–8pm; map C3 Ohel Leah Synagogue; 70 Robinson Road; tel: 2589 2650; www.ohelleah. org; Mon-Sat 7am-7.30pm; Sun 8am-7.30pm; map B4

Go for **brunch with a jaw-dropping view** on **Pearl on the Peak**'s tiny terrace

To enjoy an unadvertised treat on a Saturday or Sunday, head up to **Pearl on the Peak** for a brunch that is very fairly priced for its quality and location. Take your seat on the understated wood-decked terrace or by a window indoors, and revel in the glorious views.

Brunch starts at HK$288 for two courses, and the menu bursts with appeal. Reflecting the à la carte menu by reputed Australian chef Geoff Lindsay, light options are listed alongside refined breakfast fry-ups – from beefsteak topped with scrambled egg and cheese polenta chips, to pan-fried sea bass with chanterelle mushroom, and lobster linguine with tomato seafood sauce. A modestly priced add-on allows free flow of sparkling or still wine or juices.

Or try a select weekend brunch at one of the other international restaurants and cafés overlooking Hong Kong at The Peak. **Café Deco** serves a good one on Sundays, featuring breakfast dishes cooked to order, plus a Western and Asian hot and cold buffet, and a choice of unlimited soft or alcoholic drinks.

Half a day can be pleasantly whiled away up here. Keep kids amused with international and local lookalikes at the small waxworks museum **Madame Tussauds**, then take a bus or minibus back down for a white-knuckle ride along snaking, hill-hugging roads.

Pearl on the Peak; Shop 2, 1/F, The Peak Tower, 128 Peak Road; tel: 2849 5123; map B1
Café Deco; 1-2/F, Peak Galleria, 118 Peak Road; tel: 2849 5111; www.cafedecogroup.com; map B1
Madame Tussauds; Shop P101, The Peak Tower; tel: 2849 6966; www.madametussauds.com/hongkong; daily 10am–10pm; charge; map B1

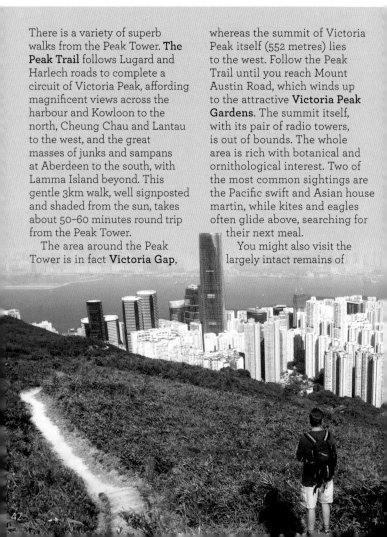

Take aim for World War II remains and lush **walking trails** on The Peak

There is a variety of superb walks from the Peak Tower. **The Peak Trail** follows Lugard and Harlech roads to complete a circuit of Victoria Peak, affording magnificent views across the harbour and Kowloon to the north, Cheung Chau and Lantau to the west, and the great masses of junks and sampans at Aberdeen to the south, with Lamma Island beyond. This gentle 3km walk, well signposted and shaded from the sun, takes about 50–60 minutes round trip from the Peak Tower.

The area around the Peak Tower is in fact **Victoria Gap**, whereas the summit of Victoria Peak itself (552 metres) lies to the west. Follow the Peak Trail until you reach Mount Austin Road, which winds up to the attractive **Victoria Peak Gardens**. The summit itself, with its pair of radio towers, is out of bounds. The whole area is rich with botanical and ornithological interest. Two of the most common sightings are the Pacific swift and Asian house martin, while kites and eagles often glide above, searching for their next meal.

You might also visit the largely intact remains of

Pinewood Battery, which lie off the more visited paths on Victoria Peak. At 307 metres, it was the city's highest coastal defence artillery platform. In the 1920s, anti-aircraft defence guns were fitted, and subsequently used during World War II. Some underground tunnels and barracks foundations remain, and information boards describe some of the missing structures.

It is possible to walk back down to Central and enjoy some of the finer views and footpaths through The Peak's wooded slopes. The **Central**

Green Trail – marked by 14 bilingual signboards highlighting points of interest – winds its way down from Barker Road, across May Road and then via paths named Clovelly, Brewin and Tramway back to the Garden Road terminus. Be prepared for the occasional steep ascent and allow around three hours for a comfortable walk up. Along the way you might see frogs, small snakes or even a wild boar.

Another short, steep route through the forest, signposted to the Mid-Levels, descends northwards from Findlay Road (just below the Peak Tower) to the beginning of the Old Peak Road. A popular longer walk descends westwards through Pokfulam Country Park, and constitutes Stage 1 of the **Hong Kong Trail**. For more ambitious hikers, the rest of the trail heads east for some 50km all the way to Tai Tam and on to Shek O. Nature-lovers can wander through forests of bamboo and fern, stunted Chinese pines, hibiscus and vines of wonderful, writhing beauty. Ornithologists log sightings of birds such as blue magpies and crested goshawks.

The Peak; map A1–B1

43

Invest in **quality wellness time** at one of the city's best **gyms and spas**

If keeping fit or being pampered is part of your holiday routine, you're in luck. Hong Kong's top-end gym and spa scene is up there with the best of them, and Central district has some serious contenders.

Pure Fitness has two gyms worth dropping into in Central, though its IFC one (Mall Level 3, Two IFC, 8 Finance Street; tel: 8129 8000; www.pure-fit. com; map E5) is more spacious; contemporary equipment, knowledgeable attendants and a clean environment make it a winner. They offer various short-term packages, too. **Fitness First** (37/F, One Exchange Square; tel: 3106 3000; www.fitnessfirst.com. hk; map E4), with other branches

around Hong Kong, is another top-end gym with day passes available.

Top spas are, unsurprisingly, found in some of the most highly rated hotels. The **Oriental Spa** (The Landmark Mandarin Oriental; 15 Queen's Road; tel: 2132 0011; www.mandarinoriental. com; map E4) is the antithesis of its mid-Central location. Book a drop-in class at the serene yoga and pilates studio; or head to the spa, heat rooms and whirlpools, set in a warm, tranquil space of natural stone and dark brown wood. Spa treatments combine eastern and western techniques, using premium essential oils.

Spa at Four Seasons (6/F, 8 Finance Street; tel: 3196 8900, www.fourseasons.com; map D5) is unusually spacious and airy. Three Chinese-themed treatments make up its 'Oriental Collection', with one using heated jade stones.

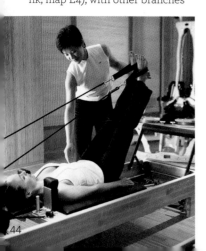

PENINSULA SPA
Over in Kowloon, a mention must go to **The Peninsula Spa by Espa** (The Peninsula hotel; Salisbury Road, Tsim Sha Tsui; tel: 2315 3322; map p.91 C1), where the attention to your needs is meticulous. Harbour-view relaxation and treatment rooms add to the experience. Don't miss the spacious steam and sauna rooms and a gorgeous colonnaded pool.

Hobnob with the **club set** at one of a handful of **members-only** establishments

A few clubs in Central allow you to mingle with Hong Kong's movers and shakers – and even though they're members-only, a good concierge can help get you in.

One of the oldest establishments is **The Hong Kong Club**, which launched in 1846 as the first colonial club in Hong Kong. Now housed in a curvaceous tower, though still on its original site overlooking Victoria Harbour and back to The Peak, members enjoy restaurants, a gym, squash courts, a billiards room and bowling alleys.

In the Old Bank of China Building (p.26), **The China Club** (pictured) is a real pleasure to visit. Its interior is a study in Shanghai Art Deco, and the walls and sculpture plinths display the art collection of its founder-owner, Sir David Tang. The Long March Bar has a wooden decked terrace with a spectacular skyscraper and harbour view.

Kee Club is a more contemporary affair, with a plush lounge, dining room and bar on the upper floors of a low-rise building. The menu is dim sum by day and Italian by night – the latter overseen by a head chef with both El Bulli and Fat Duck credentials.

The Hong Kong Club; 1 Jackson Road; tel: 2525 8251; map F4
The China Club; 13/F, Old Bank of China Building, Bank Street; tel: 2521 8888; map E3
Kee Club; 6/F, 32 Wellington Street; tel: 2810 9000; map D4

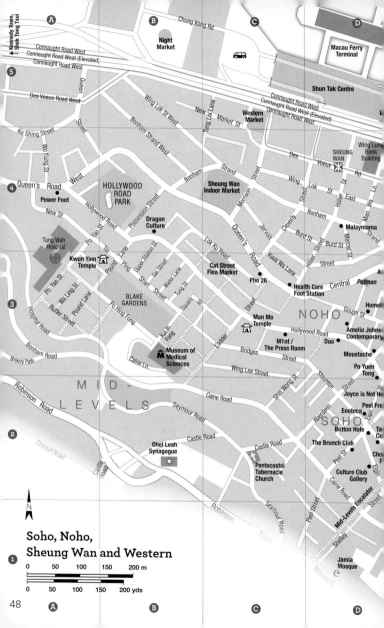

Soho, Noho, Sheung Wan and Western

0	50	100	150	200 m
0	50	100	150	200 yds

N

48

Kennedy Town, Shek Tong Tsui

Chung Kong Rd

Night Market

Macau Ferry Terminal

Connaught Road West
Connaught Road West (Elevated)
Connaught Road West

Shun Tak Centre

Des Voeux Road West

Connaught Road West
Connaught Road West (Elevated)
Connaught Road West

Western Market

Queen's Street

Wing Lok St West

New Street

Market St

Ko Shing Street

Wo Fung Street

Bonham Strand West

Tung Loi Lane

SHEUNG WAN

Des Voeux Rd

Wing Lung Bank Building

Queen's Road West

HOLLYWOOD ROAD PARK

Bonham Strand

Sheung Wan Indoor Market

Strand

Wing Lok Street

Bonham

Hillier

Mercer

Wa

Strand

Power Foot

New St

Hollywood Road

Morrison Street

Jervois Street

Burd St

Bonham

Cleverly Street

Kwai Wa Lane

Burd St

Mercer Street

Malaymama

Tung Wah Hospital

Po Yan St

Tai Ping Shan Street

Upper Station St

Sai Street

Water Lane

Lok Ku Road

Queen's Road

Hillier Street

Central

Putman

Kwun Yam Temple

Dragon Culture

Pound Lane

Cat Street Flea Market

Pho 26

Health Care Foot Station

Gough St

Homel

Po Yan St

Wa Ling St

BLAKE GARDENS

Tung St

Square St

Man Mo Temple

NOHO

Amelia Johns Contemporary

Rutter Street

Pound Lane

Po Hing Fong

Ladder Street

Hollywood Road

M1nt / The Press Room

Duo

Hospital Road

Kui In Fong

Museum of Medical Sciences

Bridges Street

Wing Lee Street

Shin Wong St

Moustache

Po Yuen Tong

Bonham Road

Caine Lane

Staunton Street

Joyce is Not He

Breezy Path

Caine Road

Peel Fre

MID-LEVELS

Robinson Road

Seymour Road

SOHO

Enoteca

Aberdeen Street

Elgin Street

Button Hole

Ta Co

Conduit Road

Castle Road

Ohel Leah Synagogue

Castle Road

The Brunch Club

Peel Street

Choi F

Castle Road

Pentecostal Tabernacle Church

Culture Club Gallery

Caine Road

Robinson

Seymour Road

Shelley Street

Mid-Levels Escalator

Jamia Mosque

Mosque St

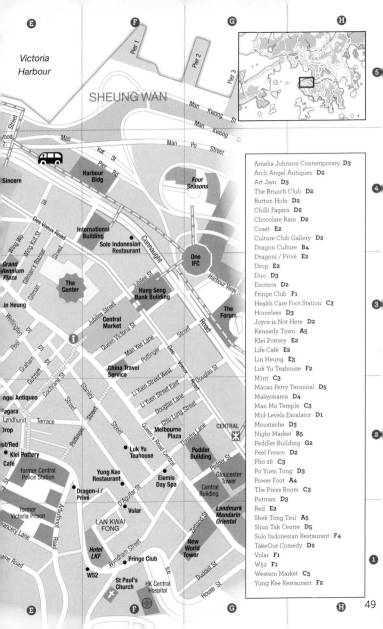

Victoria
Harbour

SHEUNG WAN

Four
Seasons

One
IFC

The
Forum

CENTRAL

Landmark
Mandarin
Oriental

LAN KWAI
FONG

New World
Tower

St Paul's
Church

HK Central
Hospital

Amelia Johnson Contemporary **D3**
Arch Angel Antiques **D2**
Art Jam **D3**
The Brunch Club **D2**
Button Hole **D2**
Chilli Fagara **D2**
Chocolate Rain **D2**
Coast **E2**
Culture Club Gallery **D2**
Dragon Culture **B4**
Dragoni / Privé **E2**
Drop **E2**
Duo **D3**
Enoteca **D2**
Fringe Club **F1**
Health Care Foot Station **C3**
Homeless **D3**
Joyce is Not Here **D2**
Kennedy Town **A5**
Klei Pottery **E2**
Life Café **E2**
Lin Heung **E3**
Luk Yu Teahouse **F2**
M1nt **C3**
Macau Ferry Terminal **D5**
Malaymama **D4**
Man Mo Temple **C3**
Mid-Levels Escalator **D1**
Moustache **D3**
Night Market **B5**
Peddler Building **G2**
Peel Fresco **D2**
Pho 26 **C3**
Po Yuen Tong **D3**
Power Foot **A4**
The Press Room **C3**
Putman **D3**
Red **E2**
Shek Tong Tsui **A5**
Shun Tak Centre **D5**
Solo Indonesian Restaurant **F4**
TakeOut Comedy **D2**
Volar **F1**
W52 **F1**
Western Market **C5**
Yung Kee Restaurant **F2**

49

Laze over **brunch** and a Sunday newspaper in **Soho**

A leisurely brunch at a Soho café or restaurant is a great way to kickstart a relaxing Saturday or Sunday. Several places serve up weekend brunches, either as a set deal or from an à la carte menu.

As its name suggests, **The Brunch Club** (70 Peel Street; tel: 2526 8861; www.brunch-club. org; map D2) makes brunch its *raison d'être*, and serves up an à la carte menu daily, and then separate lunch and dinner menus after that. Its delicious omelettes, crêpes and fresh juices make it very popular at weekends.

Life Café (10 Shelley Street;

tel: 2810 9777; map E2) serves good, wholesome vegetarian organic food throughout the week, but weekends are when the crowds assemble for its brunch dishes – scrambled tofu on wholegrain, anyone? Its juice blends, smoothies and coffees are top grade.

Another restaurant with a pretty healthy spread is Mediterranean flavoured **Duo Restaurant-Café** (118 Hollywood Road; tel: 2547 0000; map D3). Its weekend brunches include a colourful salad bar, breakfast items, starters, mains and desserts in tasting portions; priced according to how many courses you have, you can add unlimited soft or alcoholic drinks on top. Brunch signatures include steak tartare and eggs Benedict with salmon.

The Press Room (*pictured*; 108 Hollywood Road; tel: 2525 3444; www.thepressroom.com.hk; map C3) offers a popular all-day brunch at weekends from 10am till 6pm, with quality renditions of egg dishes, kippers and the like served alongside most of its regular, very appealing Continental menu. The 'raw bar' and fine wine selection are also worth investigating.

Dress to impress and hit one of Soho's **exclusive nightclubs** where top DJs take to the decks

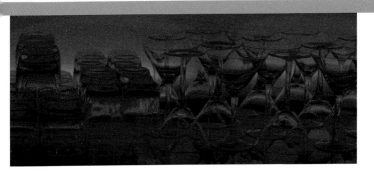

Plush decor with opulent lighting and a pumping sound system; beautifully coiffed young men and women laughing into their champagne flutes; other revellers cutting loose on a small dance floor. This scene is replayed over and over again in Soho's de rigueur nightspots.

Privé (60 Wyndham Street; tel: 2810 8199; www.prive.hk; map E2) is one of the few places where nine-litre-size bottles of champagne can be ordered. Should the cocktail of dancing, drinking and mingling stir an appetite, mini sirloin burgers and crab cakes are highlights of the snack menu.

Velvet ropes can be tough to pass at some other clubs, such as **Dragon-i** (The Centrium, 60 Wyndham Street; tel: 3110 1222; www.dragon-i.com.hk; map E2), party zone for Hong Kong's models and uber-moneyed. Regular overseas big-name DJs and occasional live musicians perform. Dance music types should head for **Volar** (Basement, 38–44 D'Aguilar Street; tel: 2810 1510; www.volar. com.hk; map F1), though, again, it sometimes gets tough on the door. The best of local and overseas DJ talent regularly spins.

M1nt (108 Hollywood Road; tel: 2261 1111; www.m1ntglobal.com; map C3), a swish club with a great bar, nightly DJ and decent-sized dance floor, gets the executive set moving. It's a members' club, allowing in those who belong to reciprocal clubs overseas or who ask very nicely on the phone. Tiny **Drop** (Basement, On Lok Mansion, 39–43 Hollywood Road; tel: 2543 8856; map E2), a very cool mini-club co-owned by a great Hong Kong DJ, Joel Lai, is easier to get into earlier in the evening. Later, its members get priority.

Take in **visual arts** by emerging talents at the **Culture Club Gallery**

A vibrant arts scene exists in Hong Kong, and you will find pockets of creativity throughout the territory. For the non-Cantonese speaker, the **Culture Club Gallery** (*pictured*) provides an accessible taster.

Launched by a local architect, Culture Club's calendar is packed with shows in all kinds of media by Hong Kong and overseas artists. As well as fine art, it holds regular salsa and music events and film screenings. Community-minded, it is succeeding in building up a regular bohemian and arts-interested bunch of loyal followers.

Downhill from here, on the edge of gallery-studded Hollywood Road and Wyndham Street, is the **Fringe Club**, which has three small galleries. These are sometimes hired out to show non-Hong Kong artists, but more often they show home-grown work by an international mix of creative residents, many of whom are not full-time artists. A champion of mostly Hong Kong-based and some regional artists is **Amelia Johnson Contemporary**, just downhill from Hollywood Road into Noho.

If you're planning to visit in March, check whether **Hong Kong Artwalk** (http://hongkongartwalk. com) is on – a night of exploring scores of galleries, with the ticket price including restaurant-donated drinks and canapés.

Culture Club Gallery; 15 Elgin Street; tel: 2127 7936; www.cultureclub.com. hk; Mon–Thur 2-10.30pm, Fri-Sat 2-11.30pm; map D2
Fringe Club; 2 Lower Albert Road; tel: 2521 7251; www.hkfringe.com.hk; Mon–Sat noon–midnight or later; map F1
Amelia Johnson Contemporary; 6-10 Shin Hing Street; tel: 2548 2286; www. ajc-art.com; Tue–Fri 10.30am-6.30pm, Sat 10.30am-6pm; map D3

Discover an Asian antique or **vintage artefact** around **Hollywood Road**

There is a slew of antique dealers on Hollywood Road and Wyndham Street, and in the main they offer genuine, politically correctly procured objects from China and Asia. Good dealers are fonts of information and should be happy to provide a certificate of authenticity from the Hong Kong Art Craft Merchants Association if you're buying an expensive piece.

Most are on Hollywood Road, which stretches from Central to Sheung Wan districts. In business for more than two decades and considered reputable is antiques shop **Po Yuen Tong** (no. 70), specialising in ceramics and bronzeware. **Arch Angel Antiques** (no. 53–5) has a large varied selection. Many pieces at **Dragon Culture** (no. 231), such as its Han

Dynasty terracotta and sculptures from other eras, are considered to be museum-quality. The gallery is now in its third decade and owner Victor Choi is a published authority on Chinese antiques.

Along Hollywood Road, a few shops and street stalls sell vintage Communist-era paraphernalia, like Mao Zedong badges, cups, copies of the *Little Red Book* and toys made of tin. In the Cat Street and Ladder Street area, just downhill from Man Mo Temple, you'll find old reproduction photos of Hong Kong and mainland China, as well as real and reproduction 'smoking posters' – collectable early- and mid-20th-century advertising prints.

Hollywood Road; map A4–D2

Feast on world food while people-watching in the atmospheric **restaurant and bar zone**

Since the Mid-Levels escalator was built in the early 1990s, all manner of shops, bars, cafés and restaurants mushroomed around it in Soho and Noho, capitalising on the captive market of standing pedestrians. Over the years, the neighbourhood has built up a reputation as an international restaurant and bar zone.

Soho's main eating and drinking thoroughfares are the first two streets parallel to and uphill from Hollywood Road: Staunton Street and Elgin Street. Both sides of these are lined with establishments, broken up occasionally by fashion or ceramic and homeware stores. In recent times, Wyndham Street has become the new kid on the block,

with its art galleries and antique shops making way for see-and-be-seen-in bars and restaurants.

On the corner of Hollywood Road where it is bisected by Shelly Street and the escalator, at the street level of a swanky tower, are two great, open-fronted bar-restaurants that are also excellent people-watching spots. Right on the corner itself is the bar of **Coast** (*pictured;* 1/F, Kinwick Centre, Hollywood Road; tel: 2544 5888; map E2); the wood decking throughout somehow feels like you're standing on the prow of a ship, cocktail or glass of wine in hand. In the restaurant, the menu is modern Australian – try the likes of grilled Pacific-Australian sea bass atop mash, with a tomato

salsa, or mini kangaroo and pork pies, packed with lean meat.

Next door, also in prime view of Soho's pedestrian flow, is **Red** (2/F, Kinwick Centre, 32 Hollywood Road; tel: 8199 8189; map E2), serving American comfort food and drinks with healthy twists. Starters include diced raw marinated Japanese scallop, flecked with fresh red chilli; meaty crab cakes; and tuna carpaccio. Of the main dishes, don't miss the 'truffled mac and cheese' – a gourmet take on a classic that packs a flavoursome wow factor.

Relative newcomer **W52** (52 Wyndham Street; tel: 6768 5252; map F1) is a three-storey Italian restaurant with a bar on the ground floor that is a lot more laid-back than many surrounding it on buzzing Wyndham Street. The great cocktails and wines by the glass are matched by fine cuisine.

You won't go short of Chinese food round here either. **Chilli Fagara** (51A Graham Street; tel: 2893 3330; map D2) has been offering Sichuan provincial dishes, with their mouth-numbing pepper-enhanced seasoning, to great acclaim for several years. Try its award-winning Pearl of the Orient: a grain-fed chicken breast is used to wrap and preserve the sweetness and juice of a long-an fruit, which is similar to a lychee. Grab a beer served traditionally, in a ceramic bowl rather than a glass.

Enoteca (47 Elgin Street; tel: 2525 9944; map D2), a tapas specialist with a very respected European wine list, is another established favourite.

Soho, Noho, Sheung Wan and Western

Be entertained with **music, comedy** and other live performances at a small **Soho venue**

A few years ago, a night of live entertainment in Hong Kong meant waiting for one of the annual arts festivals to come around, sporadic visits to a large auditorium for mainstream productions, or taking in a smaller show at the **Fringe Club** (*p.52*; 2 Lower Albert Road; tel: 2521 7251; www.hkfringe.com.hk; Mon–Sat noon–midnight or later; map F1). Housed in the various buildings of an old colonial dairy, the Fringe remains one of Hong Kong's foremost centres for alternative arts, with a small theatre and studio, and a bar stage that hosts musicians on weekend nights, but it has been joined by other small-scale venues and arts spaces in the neighbourhood.

Peel Fresco Music Lounge (49 Peel Street; tel: 2540 2046; www.peelfresco.com; map D2) has carved out a niche for itself as a jazz and blues bar – and it attracts the best of a core of respected Hong Kong jazz musicians. International musicians drop in for gigs from time to time, and are heavier in numbers during the annual music festival held here every November.

A few doors along the same street is arty bar and café **Joyce is Not Here** (38–44 Peel Street; tel: 2851 2999; www.joycebakerdesign. com; map D2), where Wednesday evening is poetry night and Thursday is music jam night; there are live music performances on Fridays, and Sunday is film night, with films projected onto a 216cm screen. Monday nights are members only.

Local stand-up comedians have been making their mark since the late 1990s at **TakeOut Comedy** (*pictured;* Basement, 34 Elgin Street; tel: 6220 4436; www.takeoutcomedy.com; map D2). Most nights have English-language comic and improvisation acts, with occasional appearances by Cantonese performers.

Get creative in **Soho and Noho** – the increasingly bohemian parts of town

Hollywood Road, Soho and Noho are strewn with art galleries, antique shops and a smattering of edgy boutiques. Within this hub of creativity, it's possible to roll up your sleeves and leave your own artistic stamp at a neighbourhood art studio.

Popular for more than a decade, **Art Jam** offers up a stretched canvas, acrylic paints and an assortment of brushes and palette knives. Don an apron and join the mixed local and foreign-resident crowd, usually an interesting bunch. Painting sessions are often themed; though no one is forced to stick to this, it makes for more camaraderie as the music plays, and cups of tea, coffee or stronger – in evening jams – are downed.

Newer kid on the block, **Art Live**, offers weekly life painting or drawing sessions – specify your preference when you book. Paints are acrylic here too; drawing includes a watercolour option as well as charcoal or pencil. Drinks and snacks are also supplied before a two-hour session of short poses, ending with a longer one. You need to be 18 or older to join in.

If 3D art is more your thing, get behind a wheel at **Klei Pottery Studio**. You may want to book more than one three-hour session with the studio owner, to build up your cup, bowl or vase, then fire, glaze and fire it again.

Art Jam; 123 Wellington Street; tel: 2541 8816; www.artjamming.com; Tue–Fri 2–6pm, 7–11pm, Sat 8pm–1am, Sun 2–6pm; map D3
Art Live; Hollywood Road, address supplied upon inquiry; email: artlivehk@gmail.com
Klei Pottery Studio; 2/F, 24 Hollywood Road; tel: 2526 8567; www.welcome.to/ klei; Wed, Fri 2–5pm, Tue, Fri 6–9pm, Sat 10am–1pm, 2.30–5.30pm; map E2

Tuck into **robustly flavoured fare** at a classic Cantonese teahouse

The Cantonese live to eat, and it is impossible to ignore the major role that food and everything around it plays in the lives of locals. A number of long-established Cantonese restaurants, with their no-nonsense decor and old-fashioned menus, are still going strong. A handful of these unpretentious places are referred to as teahouses; they serve hearty dim sum with tea from breakfast till late lunchtime, but they also have à la carte menus full of Cantonese classics. In contrast to the bright, plastic-looking, moderately priced local restaurant chains, teahouses offer dishes that have been house specials for years, served up by waiters who have long been part of the furniture.

An enduring favourite is **Lin Heung**, with its tall ceiling, strip neon lighting and tiled floor that does nothing to dull the sound of the animated dining room. The fare is tasty soups, seafood, poultry and meat dishes. Recommendations include bean curd, pork and vegetable soup; steamed razor clam with garlic; and braised aubergine with minced pork.

Heading into Central, **Yung Kee** is famous for its roast meats: goose, duck, chicken and pork with rice and vegetables are a cut above many other kitchens – notice the constant takeaway queues. Decor here has been upgraded in recent years, and it's now pretty cosy.

Nearby, narrow multi-level **Luk Yu Teahouse** is most animated at lunchtime, when dim sum and other dishes can be enjoyed in wood-panelled comfort.

Lin Heung; 160–164 Wellington Street, Sheung Wan; tel: 2544 4556; map E3
Yung Kee, 32–40 Wellington Street, Central; tel: 2522 1624; www.yungkee. com.hk; map F2
Luk Yu Teahouse; 24–26 Stanley Street, Central; tel: 2523 1970; map F2

Check out some of **Soho and Noho**'s **chic boutiques**

As with the bar and restaurant scene in Soho, the Mid-Levels escalators led to the emergence of some interesting little shops, either visible from or very near the snaking metal staircase. An adjacent cluster of streets in Noho has seen a more recent gentrification, too. Few original businesses are left, as chic clothing and furniture shops nuzzle beside small cafés with tables on the pavement.

The original menswear on display at **Moustache** (31 Aberdeen Street; tel: 2541 1955; map D3) is designed and made by the small label. Designs span 1950s- to 1970s-style suits, jacket and trouser separates, and shirts, in a spartan space with framed vintage Hong Kong and Chinese maps and prints. **Button Hole** (58–60B Peel Street; tel: 2899 2069; map D2) has an ever-changing stock of international fashion label overruns that are a rung further up the chic ladder than the shops on Johnston Road in Wan Chai.

Chocolate Rain (34 Staunton Street; tel: 2975 8318; www. chocolaterain.com; map D2) is one of a handful of jewellery and accessories shops in the vicinity. This one is particularly whimsical, with handmade bags, necklaces and other pieces coming together to tread a fine line between shop and art space.

One of Noho's eye-catchers is **Homeless** (29 Gough Street; tel: 2581 1880; www.homeless.hk; map D3), a lighting, furniture and homeware shop. It has a few other branches around town; this one also has a basement café.

Free the flow of your vital energy – or *qi* – with a **foot or body massage**

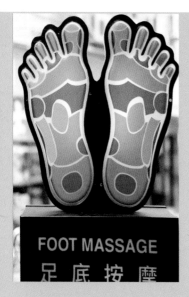

FOOT MASSAGE
足 底 按 摩

Western health treatments abound in Hong Kong, but while here, it is worth trying things the Chinese way. Pressure-point massage techniques used by traditional practitioners in Hong Kong are a far cry from Western aromatherapy. If you see a sign displaying the sole of a foot, sometimes dissected with lines into labelled areas, with no English, chances are this is an acupressure centre. A traditional reflexologist will massage your feet to boost circulation and free the flow of the *qi*, or vital energy. Full-body

treatments follow meridian points believed to run the length of the body. You can request how firmly you'd like to be massaged, but take as much pressure as you can bear – the after-effects are worth it. Treatment can be carried out through clothing provided or through a sheet.

Establishments in Sheung Wan are clean, but spartan places with bright lights and curtained-off beds. Some have bilingual price lists for treatments; generally, expect to pay around HK$120 or so for a foot massage and up to HK$200 for a body massage.

Power Foot, at the Sheung Wan end of Hollywood Road, is such a place. Some English is spoken, and tea or water is served first to allow you a few minutes' wind-down. The matronly practitioners here know their pressure points. Another is **Health Care Foot Station**, where, against a backdrop of Chinese medicinal wall charts, staff also offer shorter shoulder, hand and neck massages.

Power Foot, 88 Queen's Road West; tel: 2915 2298; map A4
Health Care Foot Station; Shop 2B, Ground Floor, Hillier Building, 273-277 Queen's Road Central; tel: 3488 6108; map C3

Stroll Sheung Wan and Western district's pungent streets of **dried goods suppliers**

Hong Kong merchants touting similar wares have a tendency to congregate cheek by jowl. In Kowloon, there are streets lined with pet shops or dedicated to sports shoe shops; and on both sides of the harbour the streets are filled with furniture-makers. For years, though, there has only been one neighbourhood devoted to dried foodstuffs and medicinal suppliers. Peddlers of these intriguing and pungent items crowd **Queen's Road West**, **Wing Lok Street**, and side streets off both, all the way west from Sheung Wan to Sai Ying Poon, just short of Kennedy Town. Walk along either and you'll see all manner of natural products being loaded and unloaded from lorries outside open store fronts that are stacked with tubs and sacks of dried beans, seeds, mushrooms, seafood and less familiar ingredients. They are used for traditional Chinese medicine (TCM), tonic drinks, and in Cantonese cooking.

Interspersed between the larger traders are small TCM practitioners, who don't have far to go to replace stock; some have a pot or two of prescribed herbs simmering in earthenware pots, in preparation for customers.

Queen's Road West; map A4–B4
Wing Lok Street; map B5–C4

UNUSUAL INGREDIENTS

It may surprise you to see the likes of dried sea horses and starfish displayed under glass – these have been prized medicinal and soup ingredients for centuries. In today's ecologically aware times, it may still be possible to spot a jarring ingredient or two: shark's fin being one.

Shop for silks, linens and handicrafts or have a drink in the handsome red-brick **Western Market**

Since few Hong Kong buildings with history have been spared the demolition ball, the striking **Western Market** building is a pleasure to behold. On a busy Sheung Wan street and right next to a pedestrian walkway that crosses multi-laned Connaught Road, this handsome red-brick colonial building is a beacon of tasteful calm.

Built in 1906, it had become the worse for wear after some eight decades operating as a food market, but a series of renovations in the 1990s restored it to its former glory – though it was still little more than a hodgepodge of shops and stalls on the ground floor and upper level. Thankfully, a further makeover in 2003 brought back a sense of the building's market origins, with a string of quality fabric vendors selling everything from Chinese silk to Harris tweed – they moved here when the legendary 'Cloth Alley' bazaar on Wing On Street was closed down to make way for high-rise office towers. Prices are fair, and the merchants (who can also tailor) know their stuff.

Other arrivals included Cantonese restaurant **The Grand Stage** (tel: 2815 2311) upstairs, enlivened by afternoon 'tea dances', and **Das Gute** (tel: 2851 2872), a bakery and Western-style café on the ground floor.

Also downstairs are shops selling arts, crafts, jewellery, toys, and some decent Hong Kong gifts and souvenirs. Shops and restaurants all keep different operating hours.

Western Market; 323 Des Voeux Road; www.westernmarket.com.hk; map C5

Get **a taste of Asia** at an authentic, no-frills **Sheung Wan** restaurant

While Soho has an abundance of stylish cosmopolitan restaurants, some more authentic, if less well dressed, ethnic establishments await in Sheung Wan.

Off the otherwise anonymous commercial stretch of Connaught Road, almost directly opposite the Macau ferry terminal, is **Solo Indonesian Restaurant**. The *gado gado* salad starter is fresh with crispy prawn crackers; the satay skewers consistently good; and the tender beef Rendang stew is fragrant. Plus, draught beer is served by the pint. Service is minimal, but you are left alone to enjoy your meal, unlike at some hurried table-turning restaurants.

Another satisfying Asian menu can be had at **Malaymama**, serving both Malay and Singaporean cuisine. Noodles are a mainstay here. Try *mie goreng* – Malay fried noodles with a choice of chicken, shrimp or beef, chopped vegetables, and topped with a fried egg. Or for a hearty noodle soup order a Singaporean *laksa*, with a spicy coconut milk base and a choice of toppings. Prices are very reasonable here.

Flavour and good value are also hallmarks of **Pho 26**, named in part after the Vietnamese national dish of rice flour noodles and slivers of beef in a broth chock-full of fresh herb leaves and chopped spring onions. Other Vietnamese dishes are also served here, such as spring rolls and fried noodles.

Solo Indonesian Restaurant; 1/F, San Toi Building, 137–139 Connaught Road Central; tel: 2541 0995; map F4
Malaymama; 11A Mercer Street; tel: 2542 4111; map D4
Pho 26; 302 Queen's Road Central; tel: 2866 1888; map C3

Appease Buddhist deities at the **Man Mo Temple**

On the corner of Hollywood Road and Ladder Street is the wonderfully dark and atmospheric **Man Mo Temple**, built around 1842 on what must have been a little dirt track. Tourists regularly throng Man Mo, but this doesn't prevent regular worshippers visiting to fill the temple with thick smoke from their joss sticks. The immense incense spirals hanging from the ceiling can burn for weeks.

Man is the god of civil servants and of literature, and in Mandarin society, civil servants were the best-educated and most sophisticated group. Mo is the god of martial arts and war, and is more popularly known by his worshippers as Kuan Ti or Kuan Kung. Statues of the legendary Eight Immortals stand guard outside the temple; inside, two solid-brass deer (representing longevity) adorn the main chamber. Near the altar, there are two sedan chairs encased in glass. Years ago, when the icons of Man and Mo were paraded through Western on festival days, they were transported on these chairs.

Man Mo Temple; 126 Hollywood Road; tel: 2540 0350; daily 8am–6pm; free; map C3

STREET SHRINES
Street shrines are rare in Hong Kong these days, as unaccounted-for urban nooks are generally reclaimed as the city constantly develops. One or two still remain, though. Look for the shrine on the steps where Peel Street meets Wellington Street (map E3). Local devotees of earth god Pak Kung burn incense sticks and coils, and leave offerings of fruit.

Ride the world's **longest** series of **covered escalators**

Hong Kong can boast a few superlatives. It has the largest seated outdoor bronze Buddha in the world (at Po Lin Monastery, *p.154*), the world's most densely populated island (Ap Lei Chau, *p.144*), and the world's longest series of covered escalators that zigzag their way halfway up The Peak. At some points the **Mid-Levels escalator** moves at street level; in other parts it soars high above it.

The escalator starts in Queen's Road Central and ends at Conduit Road in the pricey residential Mid-Levels neighbourhood. Its path through Soho accounts for the transformation of the area into one of the city's hippest zones. Canny restaurateurs and retailers realised in the early 1990s when it was built that they had a captive audience of well-heeled pedestrians to tempt with restaurants, cafés, bars and chic boutiques.

To catch a whole 23-minute leg of the escalator in one direction, you need to get your timing right. It was seemingly designed more for the convenience of the moneyed types who live in Mid-Levels, as it is in downhill-only mode for hillside commuters until 10am, travelling uphill after that

until midnight. A staircase runs parallel to the escalator, and is used by many people as a handy way to avoid crossing roads at street level.

The starting point that's easiest to find in Central is on Des Voeux Road, immediately above Central Market, where it connects with a covered walkway recently kitted out with timber and plants. It's definitely a useful way to get to Soho.

Mid-Levels escalator; map D1

65

Take the tram to its far western terminus – up-and-coming **Kennedy Town**

Since the construction of a new MTR station in **Kennedy Town** was announced in 2009, signs of gentrification are creeping into this rough cut neighbourhood – a residential and business area, with bustling shops and restaurants. The station on the new West Island Line is scheduled to open in 2014, but already some interesting cafés, restaurants and bars have opened on and around David Street, as apartment prices rise and a new breed of local and international residents moves into the area.

Ride a tram out to Kennedy Town, and take a walk along the Praya, its waterfront path, where locals exercise in the morning and evening and you can watch cargo ships come and go from the nearby terminal. After that it's time for a meal or drink – these parts are a laid-back alternative to Soho or Lan Kwai Fong, especially if you fancy international food and drink.

A relaxed meal and drink are offered at **Davis** (1 Davis Street; tel: 2818 2727), a Spanish and Asian tapas lounge bar. **The Place** (1E Davis Street; tel: 2872 0818) is a local pub with a small menu, popular with resident Westerners. A recent addition is **Al Basrah Pampa** (37 Catchick Street; tel: 2986 5455), which offers both Middle Eastern and Argentinian dishes. Highlights here are authentic meze platters, grilled Argentine steaks and decent wine.

Kennedy Town; map A5

Be spontaneous – fly to **Macau by helicopter** from Sheung Wan's Shun Tak Centre

If you fancy a spur-of-the-moment change of scene, you can make it happen within half an hour with a helicopter flight to Macau. Book a ticket on the third floor of the **Shun Tak Centre** in Sheung Wan. The flight itself is around 15 minutes, whisking you up through the towers of Hong Kong, westward above the Pearl River Estuary to the former Portuguese enclave and now Asia's Las Vegas.

Such express swiftness would depend on your timing for an available helicopter departure and, of course, you'd need to have your passport – Macau requires a separate visa (albeit free and stamped upon arrival). So do consider pre-booking. **Sky Shuttle Helicopters** leave every 30 minutes and more frequently at weekends; they start at 9.30am in Hong Kong, with the last one returning from Macau at 10.30pm.

Macau is definitely worthy of a day trip or overnight visit, with plenty of Portuguese buildings intact that date back more than four centuries. And there is also the lavish new gaming side – this market opened to overseas operations a few years ago, and big American and Australian casinos set up shop.

If you're not in such a hurry or wincing at the HK$2,400 one-way ticket price, you can take a high-speed ferry from the same building, which is also the Hong Kong to Macau ferry terminus; the journey takes just under an hour.

Sky Shuttle Helicopters; tel: 2108 9898; www.skyshuttlehk.com; map D5

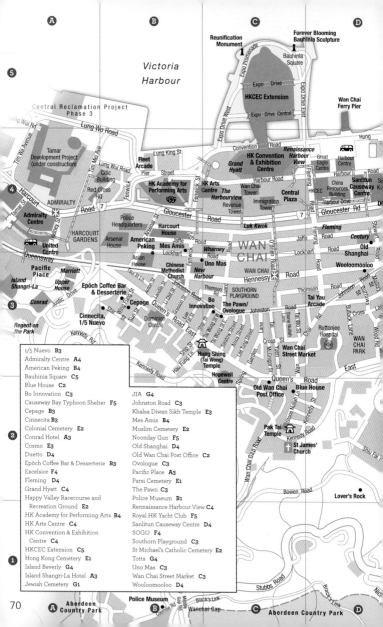

Map Labels

Victoria Harbour

Reunification Monument
Forever Blooming Bauhinia Sculpture
Expo Promenade
Bauhinia Square
Expo Drive
HKCEC Extension
Expo Drive Central
Wan Chai Ferry Pier
Central Reclamation Project Phase 3
Lung Wui Rd
Tim Wa Avenue
Tamar Development Project (under construction)
Lung Wo Road
Lung King St
Fleet Arcade
Lung Wui Rd
Tim Mei Ave
Citic Building
Red Cross HQ
Convention Road
HK Convention & Exhibition Centre
Grand Hyatt
Renaissance Harbour View
Great Eagle Centre
China Resources Building
Sanlitun Causeway Centre
Harcourt
Harcourt Road
ADMIRALTY
HK Academy for Performing Arts
HK Arts Centre
The Harbourview
Wan Chai Tower
Revenue Tower
Immigration Tower
Central Plaza
HKCEC
Harbour Drive
Gloucester Road
Admiralty Centre
HARCOURT GARDENS
Police Headquarters
Harcourt House
American Peking
Mes Amis
Chinese Methodist Church
Luk Kwok
Wharney
Uno Mas
New Harbour
WAN CHAI
Fleming
Century
Old Shanghai
Wooloomooloo
United Centre
Queensway
Arsenal House
Asian House
Jaffe Road
Lockhart Road
O'Brien Road
Hennessy Road
Marriott
Pacific Place
Upper House
Island Shangri-La
Conrad
Regent on the Park
Epoch Coffee Bar & Desserterie
Cepage
Cinnecta, 1/5 Nuevo
Justice Drive
Star St
Wing Fung St
Queen's Road
Johnston Road
Bo Innovation
The Pawn/Ovologue
SOUTHORN PLAYGROUND
Thomson Road
Tai Yau Arcade
Kennedy Rd
Dominion Centre
Queen's Road East
Tai Wo St
Swatow Street
Lee Tung Street
Spring Garden
Stone Nullah
Cross Street
WAN CHAI PARK
Ship St
Hung Shing (Tai Wong) Temple
Wan Chai Street Market
Ruttonjee Hospital
Wood Rd
Bullock Lane
Hopewell Centre
Old Wan Chai Post Office
Blue House
Pak Tai Temple
St James' Church
Queen's Road East
Kennedy Road
Stone Nullah Ln
Wan Chai Gap Road
Bowen Road
Lover's Rock
Shiu Fai
Aberdeen Country Park
Police Museum
Coombe Rd
Middle Gap Rd
Black's Link
Wanchai Gap
Aberdeen Country Park
Stubbs Rd

Index

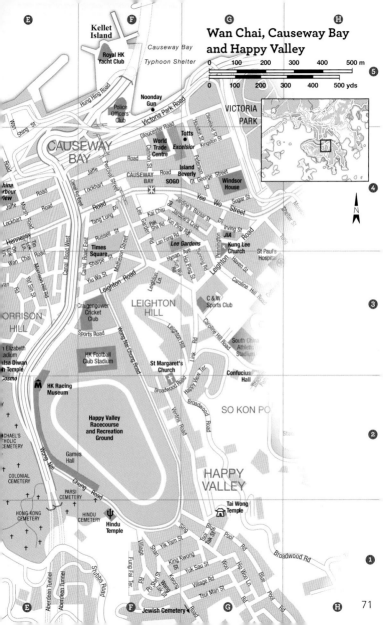

Salute the **ritual raising** of the Hong Kong and China **flags**, then have breakfast

Start the day with a Hong Kong ritual. Members of the Hong Kong Police Force officially raise and lower the Hong Kong and China flags every morning at Bauhinia Square, next to the Convention Centre building.

The ceremony takes place at 7.50am daily, lasting just under 15 minutes, to a soundtrack of the People's Republic of China's national anthem. Officers are attired in regular uniform, which changes from winter to summer. On the first day of every month, they are accompanied by a rifle unit in ceremonial dress. The ritual includes a rendition of the national anthem by the Police Band, followed by a bagpipe performance by the Police Pipe Band. On the second Sunday of each month, the ceremony is conducted by different youth groups.

Note the gold bauhinia statue (*pictured*), which represents Hong Kong's symbolic flower in bloom. While there, you can have breakfast at restaurants in the Convention Centre overlooking the square and harbour.

Bauhinia Square; Hong Kong Convention & Exhibition Centre; flag-raising daily 7.50am except in bad weather; map C5

Experience **northern Chinese food** in Wan Chai

Cantonese cuisine is everywhere in Hong Kong, and menus are pretty varied. However, it's possible to sample food from almost every other corner of China in the city's restaurants. Northern Chinese dishes from the region stretching from Shanghai to Beijing have long been popular with Hong Kong's local and international palates.

Now in its sixth decade, **American Peking Restaurant**'s name was originally concocted to attract US servicemen on R&R in Hong Kong. It is located at the quiet end of Lockhart Road, an area once peppered with girly bars – now only a few of them remain. English is understood here and the Northern Chinese menu presents an accessible choice of dishes, cooked to reliable standards. Dishes include Shanghai's famous steamed *siu long bau* dumplings of minced pork; and from the Beijing region, Peking duck and seasoned sliced beef fried in small flat bread pockets are worthy signatures. The open dining room is cosily lit and tables spaced far enough apart for privacy.

Another Northern Chinese winner in the vicinity is **Old Shanghai Restaurant** in the basement of the Century Hotel. A non-Chinese reader might miss the large Chinese-character sign outside, with very small English wording. The *siu long bau* are good here, too, as are fresh, thick Shanghai noodles, fried with a sweetish soy sauce, chopped spring onion and your choice of meat: chicken, pork or beef. The interior and staff are quite dressed-up, but as at the American Peking, most diners are casually attired.

American Peking Restaurant; 20 Lockhart Road; tel: 2527 7277; map B4
Old Shanghai Restaurant; basement, Century Hotel, 283 Jaffe Road; tel: 2827 9339; map D4

Stimulate the senses with fresh **exotic produce** at Hong Kong's **last remaining outdoor markets**

Most of Hong Kong's fresh produce markets have been moved indoors, into charmless, utilitarian multistorey buildings. Visit compact **Wan Chai street market**, near Admiralty and Wan Chai MTR stations, to see one of the few remaining collections of outdoor stalls.

If you're visiting the clothing outlet shops on Johnston Road (*see p.77*), about midway down you'll notice stalls poking out of Tai Yuen Street. This street runs down to Queens Road East; halfway along, it morphs from the cheap hosiery and kids' clothing stalls, with toy shops on both sides of the street, to vibrant fruit and vegetable stalls. Whatever is in season is displayed here – plus the imported permanent fixtures of bright pink dragon fruit, deep red lychees, oranges, mangoes and shiny red and green apples. Live seafood and meat are also sold, alongside sacks of rice and soy and other sauces. Dotted around the street market are small Thai grocery stores-cum-cafés, which primarily serve a small local community. Near the stalls are a few roast goose, duck and chicken speciality restaurants – easy to spot, as their prized ingredients hang prominently in the windows.

Still more produce is found in semi-hidden **Graham Street Market** in Soho, near Central MTR station. Here, as well as the typical selection of everyday Cantonese foodstuffs, is a smattering of flowers – all on a very small scale.

Both of these street markets were earmarked for demolition in recent years, but persistent and vocal public disapproval forced a government rethink. See them while you can.

Wan Chai street market; daily 7am–7pm; map C3
Graham Street Market; daily 7am–7pm; map p.48 D2–E3

Shoot a hoop or have fun with the family at
Southern Playground

In space-starved Hong Kong, very few strips of land remain undeveloped. Thankfully, the occasional park or tiny rest area breaks up the continual high-rises. Most districts also have indoor and outdoor sports areas, but these are often tucked away out of sight.

Southern Playground is an exception. This recreational space lies between Hennessy and Johnston Roads, slap in the centre of Wan Chai, and its marked basketball courts and hard-surface football pitch are in use day and night. Locals come here for a bit of exercise around a hoop or the goalposts; join in the fun and land a few baskets or have a kick-about. There is also a children's playground.

If you are there on a floodlit weekday evening or at the weekend, there may well be a competitive league football game on. The crowd can get pretty animated and the atmosphere is friendly. At other times the benches in the stands are popular with retired Hong Kongers, who take hot drinks and snacks there to play board games and chat.

If you want to play a racquet sport, book a court at one of scores of government-run centres across Hong Kong. Search available ones at www.lcsd.gov.hk, where bookings and payments can be made; you can use your passport to register. It also lists public pools.

Southern Playground; map C3

75

Kick back at an **outdoor café or restaurant** near the **Wan Chai ferry pier**

The Wan Chai ferry terminal (*pictured*), with its Star Ferry connection to Tsim Sha Tsui and Hung Hom in Kowloon, was something of a dead area a few years ago. Despite being just off the waterfront, there were only a few unremarkable indoor restaurants without views.

Now, a clutch of new places have sprung up, and while not all have a view, all do have tables outside. Several are on the first floor of the **Sanlitun Causeway Centre** (28 Harbour Road), rubbing shoulders with each other on a kind of elevated zigzagging dining piazza. **Green** (shop 7; tel: 2802 0666) serves up popular Thai and Vietnamese cuisine; like all restaurants here, it has a set lunch menu targeted at the office crowd, and its à la carte menu features authentic curries and grilled seafood. Popular too is **Mr Steak** (shop 10; tel: 2802 1128), a branch of the moderately priced Western-style steakhouse and grill chain; its reliable menu and landscaped terrace are appealing, and it is a good spot to watch the expenses-lunch brigade at work.

Up a notch in quality and price is **Jack's Terrazza Ristorante** (shop 8; tel: 2827 1687), with its raw oysters displayed on

ice, plus quality pasta, fish and meat dishes, and live musicians performing at night.

With the same view but from inside, three minutes west at the **Grand Hyatt** (1 Harbour Road; map C4), is **The Grand Café** (lobby level; tel: 2588 7722). Health-conscious items include the Grand Café salad with grilled salmon or beef tenderloin, and Cantonese home-style steamed cod.

Sanlitun Causeway Centre; map D4

Root for **designer bargains** at Johnston Road's **cut-price clothing outlets**

Hong Kong Island and Kowloon used to have several areas where lucky browsers at clothing outlets might bag a designer label bargain from last season. Few remain now in Tsim Sha Tsui's Granville Road, but check out the 10 or so busy, open-fronted clothing stores in Wan Chai's **Johnston Road**.

Names such as **Sample King**, **Super Sample** and **Westwood** indicate you're in the right place; these joints take payment in cash only, and none has a telephone number. Devote some time to rooting through the wares: clothes are hung on packed rails, and the cheapest items are piled into cardboard boxes that spill out onto the pavement or line long counters at the front of the shops. You may be surprised at the label bargains that pop up, including those made for UK, US and Australian department stores that don't have a retail presence in Hong Kong. Lesser-known brands of adult and kids' clothing are also on offer. Once you have trawled a few stores you may notice that the same items appear in two or three of the shops.

Johnston Road; map C3

JOHNSTON ROAD RESTAURANTS

In the same street as these cut-price outlets, the heritage building with colonial arched windows at no. 62 has been renovated to house two worthy restaurants with bars attached. **The Pawn** (tel: 2866 3444; www.thepawn.com.hk), with a name reflecting the building's original incarnation as a pawn shop, serves British gastro-pub fare and dark beers, and has great balcony tables. **OVOlogue** (*pictured;* tel: 2527 6088; www.ovologue.com.hk) is on the ground floor, with a modern take on Chinese food and cocktails, plus a furniture shop.

Catch a show, film or exhibition at the **Hong Kong Arts Centre**

Be it Chinese or Western, the arts are a significant and growing part of the Hong Kong landscape – the amount of exhibitions, performances and arts festivals has doubled in the past two decades.

Opposite the waterfront, not far from the Wan Chai Ferry pier, the multi-purpose **Hong Kong Arts Centre** (pictured) is a long-established champion of the arts. Fine art exhibitions, often quite cutting edge, are held here in an unusually spacious two-storey gallery space. Two theatres, including the intimate MacAuley Theatre, house various stage productions. There is a small cinema, and a local short film festival is one of its annual highlights. You can also enjoy the harbour-view café and restaurant, and the bookshop.

Next door is the **Hong Kong Academy for Performing Arts**, where many of Hong Kong's singers and dancers are trained. In recent years its theatre has hosted a string of Australian productions of popular musicals, as well as family shows from the UK.

The cultural scene is set to surge again, with the forthcoming West Kowloon Cultural District in the brainstorming stages.

Hong Kong Arts Centre; 2 Harbour Road; tel: 2582 0200; www.hkac.org.hk; map C4
Hong Kong Academy for Performing Arts; 1 Gloucester Road; tel: 2584 8500; www.hkapa.edu; map B4

Wine and dine the night away in trendy Star Street

In the late 1990s, regeneration hit the **Star Street** area of Wan Chai, which despite its address is a little closer to Admiralty. A cluster of low-rise car mechanics, workshops and flats were snapped up, and gleaming new towers appeared a few years later, with a couple of world-class restaurants at the ground level of gated luxury apartment blocks.

Cinnecittà (9 Star Street; tel: 2529 0199) was the first to open, with its modern white interior drawing a well-heeled crowd. You'll pay a premium, but the pastas and risottos are phenomenal and it has a great wine list – the glass-walled cellar is a decorative feature. At the same address is **1/5 Nuevo** (tel: 2529 2300), pronounced One Fifth Nuevo. You can enjoy good tapas here, but it is primarily a wine and cocktail bar attracting a glamorous mix of regulars.

The small roads off Star Street are now sprinkled with restaurants, bars and cafés. The most gourmet experience has to be **Cepage** (23 Wing Fung Street; tel: 2861 3130). The warmly lit, three-storey restaurant serves contemporary French haute cuisine. A meal here is particularly special, and priced accordingly.

Epöch Coffee Bar & Desserterie (12–14 Wing Fung Street; tel: 3525 1570) serves good coffee, pastries and desserts, plus breakfasts, fresh pasta and salads. It becomes a bar from early evening.

Star Street; map B3

Visit the charming **Old Wan Chai Post Office**, then **walk the Green Trail**

YEAR OF THE HORSE
$2.50

中國香港
HONG KONG, CHINA

Rampant redevelopment has meant that there are precious few bricks-and-mortar remnants of Hong Kong's past, but Wan Chai is one area where a few buildings recall earlier eras. The **Old Wan Chai Post Office** began life in 1912, serving as a police station for three years before becoming a post office – though it stopped operating as such in 1992, so don't expect to send a postcard. The counters, wood-beamed ceiling and wall of personal mailboxes

have been restored to how they were a century ago. It is now an environmental resource centre, and visitors are welcome; it holds children's crafts courses, using recycled materials, on Sundays, and a small, peaceful garden houses models and information boards on renewable energy.

After admiring the listed building, climb the steep path behind it up to the **Wan Chai Green Trail** for a taste of sub-tropical foliage and a view over much of Hong Kong Island. The 1.5km trail is clearly marked and has information on the flora and fauna, before ending at Wan Chai Gap Park, where taxis and buses can return you to the city buzz.

Old Wan Chai Post Office; 221 Queen's Road East; tel 2893 2856; Mon, Wed–Sun 10am–5pm; map C2

THE BLUE HOUSE
One of the last surviving examples of a typically Hong Kong style of balconied tenement building, the **Blue House** (72–74A Stone Nullah Lane; map C2), is just around the corner from the Old Wan Chai Post Office. In 2007, in response to public outcry over demolition plans, this and eight other nearby buildings constructed during the 1920s were saved and underwent renovation.

80

Taste some **authentic tapas** in the heart of the **Lockhart Road** buzz

Rightly regarded as a dining Mecca, Hong Kong is home to endless restaurants (more than 11,500 at last count), most serving up regional Chinese cuisine and pan-Asian menus. As recently as the early 1990s, there was little that could be called authentic Western cuisine in independent restaurants, and apart from in hotels, the first kitchens that took on Western fare adapted it to perceived local tastes. Since the mid 1990s, though, one-off restaurants began branching out in overseas cuisines: now hundreds of respected European, Australian and American establishments exist.

Not all are run by natives of the cuisine served, but more recent addition **Uno Mas Barcelona Tapas and Bar** was founded by a hands-on Valencian couple, who brought in a star chef from their home city. Portions are very generous for tapas, and classics such as fried chorizo and prawns sautéed in garlic go down well with a bottle of cava or house sangria, which comes in less common rosé and white mixes. It's situated in the heart of Lockhart Road's strip of open-fronted pubs, colourful discos and girlie bars; get a glimpse of all the action from the first-floor windows.

On the opposite side of the road is perennial expat favourite **Mes Amis**. The lively street-level bar gets animated from happy hour onwards on most nights – but particularly at weekends, when a DJ entices the crowd onto a small dance floor from about 10pm. Tapas are also served here, but it's more about the drinks and party atmosphere.

Uno Mas Barcelona Tapas and Bar; 2/F, 54–62 Lockhart Road; tel: 2527 9111; www.arcanatables.com; map C3 Mes Amis; 83 Lockhart Road; tel: 2527 6680; www.mesamis.com.hk; map B4

Seek out some of Asia's **sassiest clothing** in **Causeway Bay**

Shoppers from all over Hong Kong flock to **Causeway Bay** for its Japanese department stores, and scores of hip boutiques that stock international designer clothing including lesser-known Japanese and Korean fashions.

The **Island Beverly** is the centre for cool threads and accessories shopping. An escalator whisks you from the street to the first few floors, where a labyrinth-like mall of narrow corridors circuits around tiny, trendy boutiques. It's mainly womenswear on sale here, with some gents' T-shirts and footwear. Although much is sourced from overseas, Island Beverly is also home to local fledgling designers.

Aimed at a late-twenties crowd, **Narcisse** (shop 179, 1/F) designs dressy evening gowns which are custom-fitted. Popular for its costume necklaces and retro-style hair bands and brooches from Korea is **Image Code** (shop 260, 2/F). Not many stores open before midday. The centre's higher floors are home to restaurants.

Just opposite the Island Beverly, iconic Japanese department store **SOGO** offers a massive selection of audiovisual equipment, clothing for all ages, suitcases, bags, and just about anything you might need – everything is of pretty high quality. The basement has a good supermarket and fast-food outlets.

Behind SOGO, the Causeway Bay end of Lockhart Road has a string of fashionable local and Korean import boutiques.

Island Beverly; 1 Great George Street; map G4
SOGO; 555 Hennessy Road; tel: 2833 8338; www.sogo.com.hk; map F4

Hear the **Noonday Gun** sounded alongside **Causeway Bay Typhoon Shelter**

At the water's edge, one main road away from the dynamic heart of Causeway Bay, is **Causeway Bay Typhoon Shelter**, built to provide cover for the boats moored there. Live-aboard floating homes used to dock there until the early 1990s; now it's a parking spot for pleasure cruisers.

Right alongside the shelter is the **Noonday Gun**, site of possibly the last remaining colonial ritual in the territory. For the sake of tradition, despite the transfer of Hong Kong's sovereignty in 1997, an ex-British naval cannon is still fired as a time-check every day at noon.

A gun has been mounted here since the 1860s, but the idea preceded that: old British trading firm Jardine's used a cannon to salute the arrival of company directors to their warehouse area on another part of Hong Kong Island. The Royal Navy took exception to this, believing such a mark of respect should be reserved only for top government officials, and consequently ordered Jardine's to fire its gun as a daily time signal at noon as a form of punishment. Noel Coward immortalised the ritual in his 1930s song *Mad Dogs and Englishmen*.

At the other end of the typhoon shelter is the **Royal Yacht Club**, which can only be visited if you have reciprocal access through an overseas sailing club. Interestingly, this is the only Hong Kong organisation to have retained the 'Royal' moniker; after 1997 it disappeared voluntarily from other non-government establishment names.

Noonday Gun; 281 Gloucester Road; daily midday; free; map F5

Splash out on a **sundowner** or a meal with a **million-dollar view**

Victoria Harbour framed by glitzy towers is Hong Kong's quintessential backdrop, and a few restaurants and bars have both outdoor and indoor areas with spectacular harbour vistas.

In Causeway Bay at **The Excelsior** hotel, **Totts** *(pictured)* is a restaurant and cocktail lounge with a killer panoramic view, and recently opened its Roof Terrace. Tables next to its glass wall look out across the skyscraper-studded shore from Causeway Bay to Central. Enjoy a cocktail and mini kebabs from the bar menu; or a full Western meal out here or indoors.

In Wan Chai, also on a high floor with a glass-surrounded terrace and dining room, is Australian **Wooloomooloo Steakhouse**. It serves up great wines and cocktails perfect for a city sunset on its wood-decked outdoor area.

Also in Wan Chai, providing lower-level but still excellent harbour views, **Duetto** has a long premium drinks list and serves a combination of both Italian and Indian cuisine.

Totts; 34/F, The Excelsior, 281 Gloucester Road; tel: 2837 6786; map G4
Wooloomooloo Steakhouse; 31/F, The Hennessy, 256 Hennessy Road; tel: 2893 6960; map D3
Duetto; 2/F, Sun Hung Kai Centre, 30 Harbour Road; tel: 2598 1222; map D4

Attend a floodlit **evening race** at **Happy Valley**

From September to July, there's a buzz in the air most Wednesdays on Hong Kong Island, as form guides and newspaper pundits are carefully studied ahead of the floodlit night races on turf at **Happy Valley Racecourse**. Built on reclaimed malaria-ridden marshland, Happy Valley first held races in 1846, and they proved an instant hit. Night racing was introduced here in 1973, and most visitors who attend say that this is one of the most enjoyable experiences of their time in Hong Kong.

Take a tram to Happy Valley or catch a taxi (ask your driver for a racing tip – you can then of course tip him to return the favour). Pay at the public entrance and take your place among the dynamic vocal punters. Million-dollar horses ridden by some of the world's best jockeys gallop past charged-up racing aficionados, designer-dressed tycoon couples, and local residents all looking to win, and not shy to cheer their bet on.

Computerised betting, bilingual announcements and live broadcasting on enormous screens in the grounds makes it easy to follow and take part; designated tourist areas, staffed by customer relations assistants who can help explain how to place bets and answer other questions, make it even easier.

There are reasonably priced restaurants and bars to choose from. To heighten the experience, bring your passport and buy a tourist badge for access to the members' betting halls, trackside areas and members-only food and drink outlets.

The Sunday afternoon races at Sha Tin in the New Territories see even larger crowds, with far fewer tourists (*p.124*).

Happy Valley Racecourse; Wong Nai Chung Road; tel: 1817; www.hkjc.com; evening races 7.15–9.15pm; map E2

Get a fascinating insight into the criminal mind at the **Police Museum**

Hong Kong is a famously safe city for visitors, with street and petty crime a rare occurrence. However, the police force is armed here, and Hong Kong's infamous Triad societies are at least as old as the city's colonial origins. Now and then grisly crimes are committed, and the **Hong Kong Police Museum** has recorded them – along with a history of the force.

The museum, above Happy Valley on the Peak, is divided into four sections. An orientation gallery recounts a general history of the Royal Hong Kong Police Force –

though these days it has dropped the 'Royal' – from its inception in 1844, through historical photographs, archives, uniforms, firearms and other artefacts. An unexpected exhibit is the head of the 'Sheung Shui Tiger', which was shot in 1915 after killing a policeman – yes, wild tigers once roamed the territory.

Another gallery displays rotating exhibitions, covering other aspects of the force and its history to date. These include the several speciality units – marine police, the traffic division and the dog unit – plus police stations and uniforms.

But the final two sections are the most intriguing, in a voyeuristic kind of way. The Triad Societies looks at their history, the scope of their activities and the beliefs, bizarre rituals and induction practices that are part of their folklore. The Narcotics Gallery details the narcotics problem that Hong Kong has behind closed doors; and there's a mock-up of a heroin-manufacturing laboratory.

Hong Kong Police Museum; 27 Coombe Road; tel: 2849 7019; Tue 2–5pm, Wed–Sun 9am–5pm; free; map B1

Pay your respects to immigrant notables at Happy Valley's **historic cemeteries**

In modern-day Hong Kong, less than five percent of the population is non-ethnic Chinese. Yet in its early days as a treaty port and British colony, immigrant communities accounted for a far larger portion of a society that until the 1840s was little more than a series of fishing and farming villages. At Happy Valley's historic cemeteries – representing Muslim, Catholic, Hindu, Parsee, Protestant and Jewish faiths – you can pay tribute to some of those who made a mark during the colonial era.

A good landmark to start at is the **Khalsa Diwan Sikh Temple** (371 Queen's Road; map E3) – the only Sikh place of worship in Hong Kong, built in 1901 and another pointer to the territory's multicultural nature in the 19th and early 20th centuries.

Queen's Road curves onto Wong Nai Chung Road, running alongside the Happy Valley

Racetrack. A succession of cemeteries lines the hillside above. The **Muslim Cemetery** has well-kept headstones inscribed in Arabic, Chinese and English script. Next up is **St Michael's Catholic Cemetery**; unusually for superstitious Hong Kong, some 60 graves were desecrated here in February 2010 – fortunately not beyond repair. Next comes the largest, **Hong Kong Cemetery**, the final resting place for mostly Protestants, including both government and military notables.

Lastly is the **Parsee Cemetery**, for those of the Zoroastrian faith. Wong Nai Chung Road then becomes Shan Kwong Road, where an old **Jewish Cemetery**, dating from the mid-19th century, is home to departed members of the local business families of Sassoon and Kadoorie.

Wong Nai Chung Road; map F1-F3

Kowloon

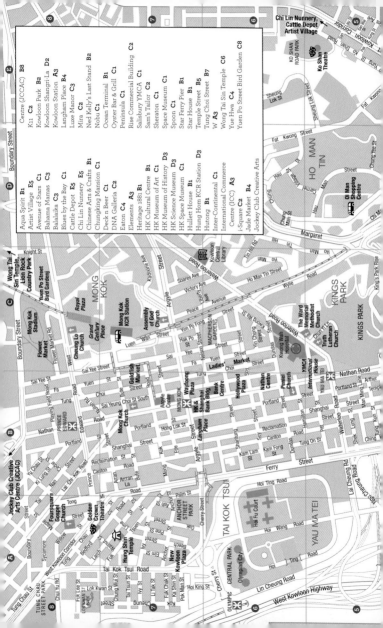

Aqua Spirit **B1**
Artist Village **E5**
Avenue of Stars **C1**
Bahama Mamas **C3**
Balalaika **C3**
Blues by the Bay **C1**
Cattle Depot **E5**
Chi Lin Nunnery **E5**
Chinese Arts & Crafts **B1**
Chungking Mansion **C1**
Deck n Beer **C1**
DNA Galleria **C2**
Eaton **C4**
Elements **A3**
Heritage 1881 **B1**
HK Cultural Centre **B1**
HK Museum of Art **C1**
HK Museum of History **D3**
HK Science Museum **D3**
HK Space Museum **C1**
Hullett House **B1**
Hung Hom KCR Station **D3**
Hutong **C1**
Inter-Continental **C1**
International Commerce Centre (ICC) **A3**
i-Square **C2**
Jade Market **B4**
Jockey Club Creative Arts Centre (JCCAC) **B8**
K11 **C2**
Kowloon Park **B2**
Kowloon Shangri-La **D2**
Kowloon Station **A3**
Langham Place **B4**
Luxe Manor **C3**
Mira **C2**
Ned Kelly's Last Stand **B2**
Nobu **C1**
Ocean Terminal **B1**
Oyster Bar & Grill **C1**
Peninsula **C1**
Rise Commercial Building **C2**
Salisbury YMCA **C1**
Sam's Tailor **C2**
Sheraton **C1**
Space Museum **C1**
Spoon **C1**
Star Ferry Pier **B1**
Star House **B1**
Temple Street **B5**
Tung Choi Street **B7**
W **A3**
Wong Tai Sin Temple **C6**
Yue Hwa **C4**
Yuen Po Street Bird Garden **C8**

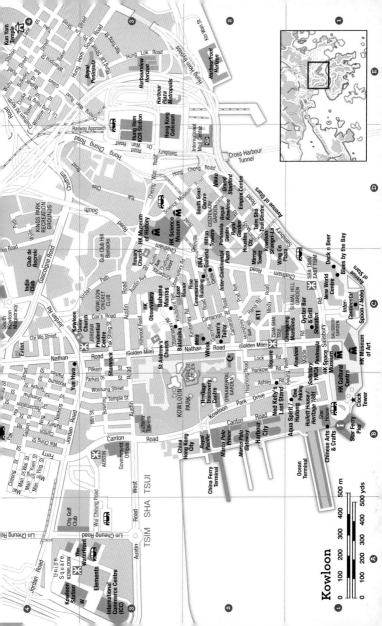

Take tea in TST – with scones or dim sum

One of the best pleasures of a visit to Hong Kong is to take a break from the clamour of streets and shops and relax with a steaming cup of freshly brewed tea. Spoil yourself in a refined refuge in Tsim Sha Tsui and take tea the English or the Cantonese way.

Warm, oven-fresh scones and finger sandwiches await in **The Lobby** at **The Peninsula** hotel (Salisbury Road; tel: 2315 3160; daily 2–7pm; map C1) which serves traditional English afternoon tea. Next door at **1881 Heritage** is another top-notch afternoon tea selection in **The Parlour** (1/F, Hullet House, 2A Canton Road; tel: 3988 0101; daily 2.30–5.30pm; map B1) where the strawberry preserve and Hullet House tea blend deserve a special mention.

The Cantonese term *yum cha* literally means 'drink tea', but it also refers to the enjoyment of a tea-fuelled dim sum meal. Two of the most refined places for *yum cha* are at **Spring Moon** in The Peninsula, a take on a Shanghai teahouse with fine dim sum and a 'tea master' who explains the differences between 25 varieties; and imperial-looking **Shang Palace** (Basement, Kowloon Shangri-La, 64 Mody Road; tel 2733 8754; map D2), where 10 premium teas are brewed with a monthly changing dim sum list.

Shop at a **space-age mall** in contemporary Kowloon

In recent years, Kowloon's newest neighbourhoods, Jordan and Tsim Sha Tsui, have seen the arrival of some futuristic mall complexes with a wider variety of brands than most older shopping centres.

Elements, atop Kowloon MTR and Airport Express stations, is one of the most spacious. Its wide corridors, displaying modern sculpture, are very easy on the eye. International fashion and sports brands, high-end home accessories and electronics stores are all housed here. Head up to its podium-level bars and cafés, where tables spill onto a piazza-like terrace bordered with potted greenery. For the adventurous or those with kids in tow, there is an ice rink on the ground floor.

The newest malls on the block, on either side of Nathan Road in Tsim Sha Tsui, are **K11** and **i-Square** (pictured). Both reflect the cyber age in their design, with lots of white space and projected lights. K11's standout stores include **Laosmiddle** (shop 215, tel: 3122 4049), a home-grown bag and shoe shop; and Japanese fashion and jewellery brand **Mukai** (shop 219, tel: 2663 9939). Restaurants are thoughtfully stacked at one end of the mall in a 'gourmet tower'.

i-Square is even more stark and minimal, aimed at a young adult shopper – designer streetwear, bags and accessories feature in abundance. **TShirt Store** (shop 402, tel: 2682 3687) sources lively tops; **New Balance** (shop 404, tel: 2947 9182) has limited-edition footwear and clothing. There are several cafés and noodle bars; for a more indulgent meal hit the upper floors. One of Hong Kong's best cinemas, **UA**, is on the seventh floor.

Elements; 1 Austin Road West; tel: 2735 5234; map A3
K11; 18 Hanoi Road; tel: 3118 8070; map C2
iSquare; 63 Nathan Road; tel: 3665 3333; map C2

Absorb the detail of ancient Chinese and colonial-era paintings at the **Hong Kong Museum of Art**

The distinctive 'skateboard-ramp'-roofed **Hong Kong Museum of Art** on the Kowloon waterfront is a great place to while away a few hours. Not only does it house some of the world's finest examples of ancient Chinese art, but it also contains hundreds of traditional and contemporary works.

Among the most fascinating artworks are a number of China Coast pieces by British-born George Chinnery (1774–1852), as well as works by several of his peers. The paintings show a 19th-century Hong Kong, Macau and Southern China far removed from their modern-day appearances, at a time when South China ports were in transition from fishing villages to trading hubs. Chinnery, who also spent time in India, painted in oil on canvas in meticulous detail.

Much of this kind of artwork at the museum is rotated, so you never know exactly what will be on show; but you might also see old engravings from British periodicals, which illustrated articles on the region in the days before photography.

Traditional Chinese art, antiquities and jewellery remain on permanent display. Nomadic pieces caricature animal motifs, such as wild cats and wolves – revered and feared on the desolate plains. Antique accessories include elaborate long court necklaces of semi-precious stone and noblewomen's headdresses. The Gold section features ornaments and jewellery that span Chinese dynasties and provinces alike.

The permanent galleries of the Xubaizhai Collection house prized examples of Chinese ink painting and calligraphy on both silk and paper. Some date back as far as the 15th century, yet are immaculately preserved. One example particularly worth tracking down is the ink-on-silk vertical scroll landscape by Tang Yai (1470–1523), a native of Suzhou (Jiangsu province), said to be one of the 'Four Masters' of the Ming Dynasty.

Contemporary Hong Kong art is also exhibited here, with a recent spate of themed exhibitions

TST MUSEUMS
Tsim Sha Tsui (TST) is the prime place in Hong Kong to visit for a museum fix; all are government-run and details can be found at www.lcsd.gov.hk/ce/museum. The **Hong Kong Museum of History** (100 Chatham Road South; tel: 2724 9042; map D3) has an attractive collection of natural, local and ethnic history exhibits – with plenty of vintage film footage in screening rooms. Next door, the **Science Museum** (2 Science Museum Road; tel: 2732 3232; map D3) has over 500 exhibits on permanent display in 18 galleries, including robotics, computers, phones and a miniature submarine, and is a popular spot for families and kids. The **Space Museum** (10 Salisbury Road; tel: 2721 0226; map C1), another kiddie fave with its unmissable planetarium dome next to the Museum of Art, screens astronomical and natural history documentaries, some in OMNIMAX Sensaround format. Its displays include interactive scale-model rockets and genuine astronaut suits.

in mixed and new media. The museum shop is one of the best places to look for art books and prints in Hong Kong.

Hong Kong Museum of Art; 10 Salisbury Road; tel: 2721 0116; www.lcsd.gov.hk/ce/museum; Fri–Wed 10am to 6pm, Sat until 8pm; charge, Wed free; map C1

Begin a Tsim Sha Tsui **bar crawl** in buzzing **Knutsford Terrace**

Knutsford Terrace, a discreet pedestrianised stretch, is one of the most popular places in Kowloon for alfresco dining, drinking and socialising. Come here to get your TST bar crawl off to a swinging start.

Bahama Mamas (nos. 4–5; tel: 2312 6222; map C3) was the original bar here, and is good for a frozen margarita. Like many of the bar-restaurants round here, it throngs through the night, particularly at weekends when tables spill out of its open front. For a quirky vodka, don the furry

hat and thick coat provided for the freezer room at Russian-themed **Balalaika** (2/F, no. 14; tel: 2312 6222; map C3).

If big band music is your thing, move on for a drink at **Ned Kelly's Last Stand** (11a Ashley Road; tel: 2376 0562; map B2), where long-serving musicians get things going after 9pm.

Deserve a splurge? **The Peninsula** hotel on Salisbury Road (map C1) houses two striking concept bars. Cosy **Salon de Ning** (basement; tel: 2315 3355) is based on the home of a fictional Art Deco-era party girl, with a string of open-fronted rooms each richly decorated in a different theme – from Alpine ski villa to canopied Arabian pavilion. Drinks-wise, try the exquisite fruit-based Hong Kong Dragon or the Ning Sling. A live band plays nightly.

Perched at the top of the hotel, with an interior by Philippe Starck, **Felix** (28/F; tel: 2366 6251) has two enclosed bar areas – one quiet, one buzzing. Pull up a Starck stool at its light-box-like Long Table *(pictured)* to take in the proceedings against a Hong Kong harbour backdrop. Bar snacks here are particularly tempting, and the restaurant's à la carte menu can also be ordered at the bars.

Browse a **lively outdoor market** for an affordable Hong Kong souvenir

So much outdoor trading in Hong Kong has moved indoors over the past decade or so, but a few remaining Kowloon outdoor markets are fun to browse.

Jade Market in Yau Ma Tei gets its fair share of tourists, but is also a local favourite for jade and other semiprecious stone jewellery. For thousands of years, jade has been associated with long life, good health and good fortune by the Chinese. Pendants, bracelets, rings and brooches in various hues are the main finds here. Traders are generally reputable – if a price is very cheap, presume it is very low-grade or not real jade.

Ladies' Market in Mong Kok is another consumer hotspot. As its name indicates, most items on sale are for women: clothing, bags, accessories and cosmetics make up the bulk of the stock. But kids' clothes, toys and household gear can all be had, at good prices.

Over in Jordan, the market most visited by tourists is **Temple Street Market** (*pictured*), and for good reason: if looking for a souvenir or present, it is hard to walk away empty-handed. Chinese-style costumes for children, T-shirts, funky watches and clocks, chopsticks sets and ornaments are all up for grabs. There are scores of restaurants around the market, and fortune-tellers reading palms and faces; and with an audio backdrop provided by CD and DVD stalls, it's a pretty lively scene.

Jade Market; Kansu and Battery Streets; daily 10am–5pm; map B4
Ladies' Market; Tung Choi Street; daily midday–11.30pm; map C6
Temple Street Market; daily 4pm–midnight; map B5

Go for an **after-dinner stroll** along the harbour promenade, and delight in the **Symphony of Lights**

The best unobstructed view of Hong Kong Island can be seen from the very tip of the Kowloon Peninsula where a wide pedestrian walkway stretches from TST's Star Ferry all the way to Hung Hom Station.

At 8pm nightly, the **Symphony of Lights** illuminates towers and the night sky on both sides of the water with LED and laser lighting effects. The best vista is from the upper viewing deck of the promenade – a raised platform with a line of benches in front of the Hong Kong Cultural Centre. If you left your tripod at home, a handful of digital image-making stalls offer reasonably priced prints.

Although more intense at night, the view is also striking by day. East of the Cultural Centre, beyond the InterContinental Hotel and New World Centre, the **Avenue of Stars** – think

handprints in cement, à la Beverly Hills – can be seen more clearly at daytime, too. Film fans should look out for prints and plaques honouring Jackie Chan, Chow Yun-Fat, Jet Li and John Woo among others, as well as a bronze sculpture of Bruce Lee.

Waterfront promenade; map B1–E2

HARBOUR REFRESHMENT
Cafés, bars and restaurants with outdoor tables make this one of the few spots in the territory for downtown harbour-side refreshment where you can actually hear the sound of the swell and passing vessels. **Deck n Beer** (tel: 2723 9227; map C1) is a relaxed people-watching spot with wooden decking; for a larger bar with an international menu, there is **Blues By The Bay** (tel: 2732 2066; map C1). Both joints are near the New World Centre, though neither has a street number.

Get fitted up for a **bargain price** in Tsim Sha Tsui

If you are more accustomed to buying clothes off the peg, Hong Kong makes it affordable to treat yourself to a perfect fit. Bespoke bargains are to be had across **Tsim Sha Tsui** at dozens of small tailors' workshops. Chinese and Indian tailors have honed these skills over generations, and their deft cutting and needlework, in the style and material of your choice, offer true value for money.

Usefully, or annoyingly, depending on whether or not you are in the market for a made-to-measure suit, shirt, dress or the like, street touts in this neighbourhood routinely approach those they presume are tourists. Don't feel obliged to listen to the sales patter – if interested, cut to the chase and ask for prices of individual garments or a package. Of course, for a true picture of what

to expect, visit the tailor to inspect samples of their work.

Testimonial letters from satisfied customers are routinely displayed – nowhere more so than at **Sam's Tailor**, where suits and dresses have been run up for many a Western and Asian celebrity.

Beware of misleading tailor touts, though; remember to check costs and materials used. Suits and dresses can be turned around in 24 hours, but allow more time if you can, as it is wise to suggest two fittings (after the initial measuring-up) before you pick up the final garment (or have it delivered to your hotel, usually at no extra charge if you're staying in or near the neighbourhood).

Sam's Tailor; G/F, Burlington Arcade, 94 Nathan Road; tel: 2367 9423; www. samstailor.biz; map C2

Find peace in the landscaped grounds of two **urban temple complexes**

In the heart of bustling Kowloon are two tranquil urban oases: **Wong Tai Sin Temple** and **Chi Lin Nunnery**.

You will know you have arrived at the Wong Tai Sin temple when you hear the sound of rattling *chim*, the bamboo sticks used for fortune-telling. Known as 'the fortune-tellers' temple', this Taoist temple complex in a natural setting at the heart of urban Kowloon is the liveliest and most colourful place of worship in Hong Kong. Constantly bustling with worshippers, it is certainly one of the most rewarding for outsiders to visit. The carvings on the rear of the main altar depict the story of the god Wong Tai Sin, a simple shepherd who is said to have been given the formula for an elixir for immortality by a heavenly spirit. There is a small entrance charge to some areas, such as the lovely **Good Wish Garden** (though this is not always open).

Flanked by a lily pond and instantly recognisable by its beautifully embellished carved wooden roofs, the huge Buddhist Chi Lin complex was built between the 1930s and 1990s, but entirely in the classic style of the Tang dynasty (AD 618–907). Its

seven wooden halls were even constructed using wooden tenons instead of nails. Nestled among the surrounding high-rise apartment blocks is the tranquil **Nan Lian Garden**, a relatively new public park also built in the Tang style. The scenic garden is meticulously landscaped over 3.5 hectares, in which every hill, rock, body of water, plant and timber structure has been placed according to specific rules and methods.

Wong Tai Sin Temple; 2 Chuk Yuen Village, tel: 2327 8141; www.siksikyuen. org.hk; daily 7am–5.30pm; free; map C8 Chi Lin Nunnery; 60 Fung Tak Road; tel: 2329 8811; www.nanliangarden.org; daily 7am–9pm; free; map E6

Treat yourself to a **gourmet feast** at one of three
top international restaurants

Celebrity chefs from overseas have been a big hit in town in recent years, and two of them have set up home under the same hotel roof at the InterContinental Hong Kong, overlooking the harbour.

Spoon by Alain Ducasse (lobby level; tel: 2721 1211), flying the flag for the global empire of the big-name French chef, is hard to beat for a quality dining experience. Here's why: superb modern French cuisine; a great wine and non-alcoholic drinks list; personal, attentive service; a relaxed, stylish environment, and the feeling that you're perched right on the edge of the harbour.

Nobu (2/F; tel: 2721 2323), headed up by king of Japanese fusion Nobu Matsuhisa, houses a more elegant dining room in its Hong Kong branch than some elsewhere. The menu concept, though, is constant: contemporary Japanese with South American accents, reflecting the years Matsuhisa spent in Peru.

Also in the neighbourhood is much-talked-about **Whisk**, run by Singapore's acclaimed young chef Justin Quek. Having trained in Michelin-starred restaurants in France, Quek's French-inspired menu, with a handful of other European and Asian influences,

is wowing diners. Prices are good value for the level of cuisine, and there is a higher chance of Quek being in the kitchen than in some big-name restaurants: he drops in every two months.

Spoon and Nobu; InterContinental Hong Kong, 18 Salisbury Road; Spoon tel: 2313 2256, Nobu tel: 2313 2323; www. hongkong-ic.intercontinental.com; map C1
Whisk; 5/F, The Mira Hong Kong, 118–130 Nathan Road; tel: 2315 5111; map C2

Snap up top-quality items from **Mainland China** at these elegant **department stores**

Some of Mainland China's best clothing, artwork and foodstuffs are shipped south to Hong Kong, and many visitors track down an item or two from the big country north of the border to take home.

Small tourist shops and some market stalls offer plenty of keepsakes, but for products that will last and whose quality will be more appreciated, there are a couple of reputable department stores worth investigating.

For silk clothing, household porcelain, tea, medicinal herbs and other top-grade products from Mainland China, **Yue Hwa**'s flagship store in Jordan is the best bet. You'll find linen tablecloths and sheets; casual and smart clothing, with Western cuts but made by some of the top Chinese brands, also feature. The art

section sells paintings and prints, sculptures and religious statues.

In Tsim Sha Tsui, **Chinese Arts & Crafts** has less homeware and only top-end clothing. It focuses on fine ornaments and jewellery: elaborate carvings of jade, crystal and other semiprecious stones are displayed on pedestals. One large jade piece, depicting the mythical nine dragons after which Kowloon is named, was recently priced at HK$8.8 million.

Both stores have other branches across Hong Kong.

Yue Hwa; 301–309 Nathan Road, Jordan; tel: 3511 2222; www.yuehwa. com; daily 10am–10pm; map C4
Chinese Arts & Crafts; Star House, 3 Salisbury Road, Tsim Sha Tsui; tel: 2735 4061; www.chineseartsandcrafts.com. hk; daily 10am–9.30pm; map B1

Peruse **cutting-edge artwork** in Kowloon's specially converted creative spaces

Contemporary fine art has seen something of a renaissance in Hong Kong. With the help of government grants, two disused industrial premises have been converted into arts spaces.

Cattle Depot Artist Village, in a scruffier part of East Kowloon, began life in 1997, when it was renovated from a slaughterhouse to workshops and galleries. Artistically inclined non-profit tenants were granted space, and visitors are welcome to visit their galleries. Art group **Artist Commune** is one organisation that settled there, building studios, holding exhibitions and events and inviting international talent to its artist-in-residency programme. Another group, **1a Space**, has carved out a reputation as a leader of Hong Kong's contemporary visual arts scene, organising activities and exhibitions, and producing publications. **Videotage** merges the concepts of video and montage, focusing on the development of video and new media art. It has held cutting-edge audiovisual exhibitions and performances.

In 2008, a larger converted factory space opened: the **Jockey Club Creative Arts Centre**, in Shek Kip Mei. The workshops of some 150 local artists, performance groups and musicians can be visited, and it has a café. There is plenty to see at JCCAC – workshops for school children, plays in rehearsal, and art taking shape in studios. **Hong Kong Open Printshop** (Room 5, 8/F; tel: 2319 1660) is one of the territory's few printmaking facilities. **The Hong Kong Puppet and Shadow Art Center** (Room 6, 13/F; tel: 3165 0958) teaches string and Asian silhouette puppet-making, and rehearses performances here.

Cattle Depot Artist Village; 63 Ma Tau Kok Road; Wed–Sun 10am–8pm; free; map E5
Jockey Club Creative Arts Centre, 30 Pak Tin Street; tel: 2353 1311; www.jccac. org.hk; daily 10am–10pm; free; map B8

Get a **bird's-eye view** over Hong Kong while savouring an exquisite **meal or cocktail**

Combining a fine meal with an elevated harbour panorama is a treat that any visitor to Hong Kong should try to lavish on themselves. If a full meal is beyond budget, most of these glamorous recommendations – all in Tsim Sha Tsui – have bar areas, where the backdrop can be enjoyed over a cocktail or two. From up here, you get a sense of how narrow most of Kowloon's streets really are – and how the pavements teem with ant-like Hong Kongers.

Aqua Spirit (*pictured;* 30/F; One Peking Road; tel: 3427 2288; www.aqua.com.hk; map B1) is one such example. Theatrically dark, to make the most of the 360-degree views of Victoria Harbour and Kowloon, it sits atop Aqua restaurant, where the menu is split into Italian and Japanese cuisine. Weekend brunch is a relaxed time to soak up the view. Book in advance for semi-private booths.

One floor down in the same building, **Hutong** restaurant (28/F, One Peking Road; tel: 3428 8342; www.aqua.com.hk) is another good spot for the nightly harbour light show at 8pm (*p.98*). Here, Northern Chinese food is served in a dark contemporary-meets-antique environment.

Oyster Bar & Grill (18/F, Sheraton Hong Kong Hotel & Towers, 20 Nathan Road; tel: 2369 1111 ext 3145; map C1) has a sophisticated yet understated ambience that lets the view do the talking and oozes 'special occasion'. Its reputable fresh oyster bar selection is joined by an always-impressive Western fine-dining menu. There is a separate bar serving a top-tier snack menu.

Philippe Starck-designed restaurant and bar **Felix** *(p.96)* offers another view from on high, from within a notable interior.

For an eye-in-the-sky splurge in a helicopter, **Heliservices**, in

NEW VIEWING PLATFORM
The 100th-floor viewing area in the **International Commerce Centre** (ICC) tower in West Kowloon (1 Austin Road West; map A3) brings panoramas previously unseen in Hong Kong. Not only is it scores of floors higher than any other, but most developers have previously been too concerned with rental yield to consider such a thing. The skyscraper's roof stands at 484 metres, and is third tallest in the world. The Ritz Carlton on the uppermost 15 floors became the world's tallest hotel in 2010.

conjunction with The Peninsula hotel (www.peninsula.com), offers some High Flyer packages, available daily, that combine a five-minute flight over the harbour in an Aerospatiale Squirrel with afternoon tea, lunch or a spa treatment. Fly & Dine packages offer a longer 15-minute helicopter ride from the hotel's rooftop, plus a meal in one of its restaurants. Prices vary according to the flights and meals selected and the number of people taking part.

Enter a warren of **hip boutiques**

Around the Chatham Road end of Granville Road is a cluster of small boutiques with attitude. The pioneer was the Beverly Commercial Building, Hong Kong's first shopping arcade catering for young hipsters, but in the last few years it has become overrun with other businesses and the mantle has been passed to **Rise Commercial Building** – a veritable warren of fashionable outlets.

Lots of the alternative fashion and lifestyle products found here are designed by young Hong Kongers. Many shops also display unique pieces that have been sourced from around Asia or beyond. Japanese and Korean clothing and footwear have been popular with the fashion-conscious for some time here. **Absolute** (no. 424) and **ing** (nos. 102–103 and 423) stock a variety of what's regionally hot. **Minimal** (no. 120) offers wacky futuristic and retro gadgets. **Mint and Tulip** (no. 424; www.mintandtulip. com), a small American jewellery-maker, has a shop here.

Near Rise Commercial Building, new **DNA Galleria** mall is chock full of trendy shops. In addition to the official main entrance address, there is also an entrance on Granville Circuit. **The Alley** (nos. 304–305) sells street wear and some spray-painted artwork by local artist SFZ (Start From Zero).

The side streets around here have plenty of interesting small outlets too, displaying an ever-changing assortment of clothes, accessories and costume jewellery. In this vicinity, many places open shop around mid-afternoon and stay trading until late.

Rise Commercial Building; 5–11 Granville Circle; map C2
DNA Galleria; 61–65 Chatham Road South; map C2

Take a **neon sign tour** along and around Kowloon's 'Golden Mile'

A century ago, Kowloon Peninsula's main artery, **Nathan Road**, was tree-lined and elegant, and its low-rise buildings were desirable residences. But since the 1960s, it has become known for the stretch of large-scale neon signage that overhangs the road and inspired its nickname The Golden Mile. It is still a spectacle today.

Stand at the end of Nathan Road in Tsim Sha Tsui. You are now looking due north along Kowloon's main artery, ablaze with colourful signs. **Big Bus Tours** (tel: 2723 2108; www.bigbustours.com) ply the route, but exploring on foot allows you to deviate onto side streets like Peking and Haiphong roads, neck craned upwards at the festival of lights. If pushed for time, walk up Nathan Road to the junction with Jordan Road, then look left – this takes no more than 15 minutes, and the orgy of neon on both streets is quite a sight.

Most signs are in Chinese characters only, and a large portion advertise Cantonese restaurants or jewellery shops. One much-repeated sign is a circle crowned by what looks like bat wings – this is the time-honoured motif for pawn shops.

Nathan Road; map C1–C3

Cross the harbour on Hong Kong's quintessential form of transport, the **Star Ferry**

From Rolls-Royce to rickshaw, Hong Kong offers every mode of conveyance. But the territory's quintessential form of transport is the Star Ferry. Shunting back and forth across Victoria Harbour between Tsim Sha Tsui and Central piers, these green-and-white ferries link the community together in a way that is both symbolic and practical.

The dozen-strong fleet would win few prizes for glamorous design. Yet the clanking gangways, weather-beaten coxswains and solid wooden decks have a timeless character and the five-minute crossing provides views that are second to none – particularly at twilight. The upper decks avoid engine-room noise and fumes.

The first of the current 'Star' fleet made their maiden voyages in 1898. Until Hong Kong Island was connected to Kowloon by road tunnel and the MTR in the 1970s, the Star Ferry was the prime way to cross the harbour – these days it is generally quicker to use the MTR.

Star Ferry also runs routes from Tsim Sha Tsui to Wan Chai on Hong Kong Island, and from Hung Hom in Kowloon to Central, and offers tours – check the website.

Around the Tsim Sha Tsui piers are a number of operators who offer harbour cruise packages by day or night, including **Watertours of Hong Kong** (tel: 2926 3868; www.watertours.com.hk). For something a little more upmarket, you might jump aboard red-sailed wooden junk **Aqua Luna** (tel: 2116 8821; www.aqua.com.hk), which offers daytime and evening cocktail cruises, sometimes with live musicians aboard.

Star Ferry; tel: 2367 7065; www.starferry.com.hk; daily 6.30am–11.30pm; map B1 and p.24 F5

Observe small-scale pets and their owners at
Bird Garden and **'Fish Street'**

Although pet dogs have become a little more popular in the last few years, in space-challenged Hong Kong smaller domestic companions – if any – are preferred. Caged birds have been popular with retirees for generations; many take their winged friends to meet other owners in parks or teahouses that permit them. Pet fish are traditionally thought to impart good energy in a home; some believe that when a fish dies, it absorbs the bad luck that would otherwise have fallen on a person living there.

Hong Kong has themed streets across its various districts, and Mong Kok is the go-to area for pet birds and fish. Following the outbreaks of avian flu, the old 'Bird Street' that traded in feathered pets was ordered to cease its function. In its place came the **Yuen Po Street Bird Garden**, which functions similarly but is regulated for hygiene. It is the favoured gathering place of Hong Kong's songbird owners, with some 70 stalls selling birds and bird-keeping paraphernalia.

Tung Choi Street is packed with goldfish, tropical fish, turtles, aquariums and everything for your aquatic pet needs. Shops open from around 10.30am until 10pm, and the area is popular with local families and kids.

Yuen Po Street Bird Garden; daily 7am–8pm, map C8
Tung Choi Street; map B7

People-watch at dynamic and multicultural
Chungking Mansions

Looking at it now, it is hard to believe that what lies behind the shambolic facade of **Chungking Mansions** was in the 1960s the height of luxury apartment living. By the 1980s it had degenerated into unkempt boarding houses, and all manner of vice went on there. The mid-1990s saw some renovation of its adjoining shopping arcade, and these days Chungking Mansions has cleaned up much of its act.

The tenement building is home to scores of Indian and South Asian restaurants – several of them have been operating for years and offer value and authenticity. The **Taj Mahal Club** (3/F, Block B; tel: 2722 5454), **Khyber Pass** (7/F, Block E; tel: 2721 2786) and **Delhi Club** (3/F, Block

C; tel: 2368 1682) are all reliable for samosas, naan bread, rice, curry, tandoor dishes, dal, lassis and a Kingfisher beer or two.

Clothing and all manner of traded goods can be bought from ground-floor wholesalers. On the same level are African traders and cafés and dessert shops that cater to halal observers. There are a couple of very reasonably priced internet cafés, as well as money-changing operations.

Do not be put off by the cast of characters that hangs around its entrance – some will immediately produce restaurant cards, presuming visitors are there for a meal. It is completely safe to visit.

Chungking Mansions; 36–44 Nathan Road; map C1/2

Leave urban Kowloon behind and hike up to
Lion Rock Country Park

Lion Rock Country Park is one of a few local city escapes that whisk you quickly from street to sky. In no time at all you can leave the bustle of traffic and pedestrians behind and reach this rugged upland region that connects North Kowloon and Sha Tin in the New Territories.

From a distance Lion Rock, the 495-metre peak which gives the park its name, really does resemble a maned head in profile. It is edged by trails both on the east and west sides – comfortable walking shoes and water are all that you need.

The park is easily reached from either Wong Tai Sin or Kowloon Tong MTR stations. It is signposted from the former, and takes around 10 minutes or so on foot; or it's a five-minute taxi ride from Kowloon Tong.

Ascend above the residential apartment blocks and once you've reached the summit you are rewarded with stunning views across Kowloon and Victoria Harbour to Hong Kong Island. Soak up the sights, listen to the birdsong and look out for the few roaming macaques up here. In some small sections of the hillside above Wong Tai Sin, local walkers have attempted to tame nature, creating their own little landscaped areas.

The more serious climber can scale vertiginous Lion Rock itself on either its east or west face.

Lion Rock Country Park; map C8

111

New Territories

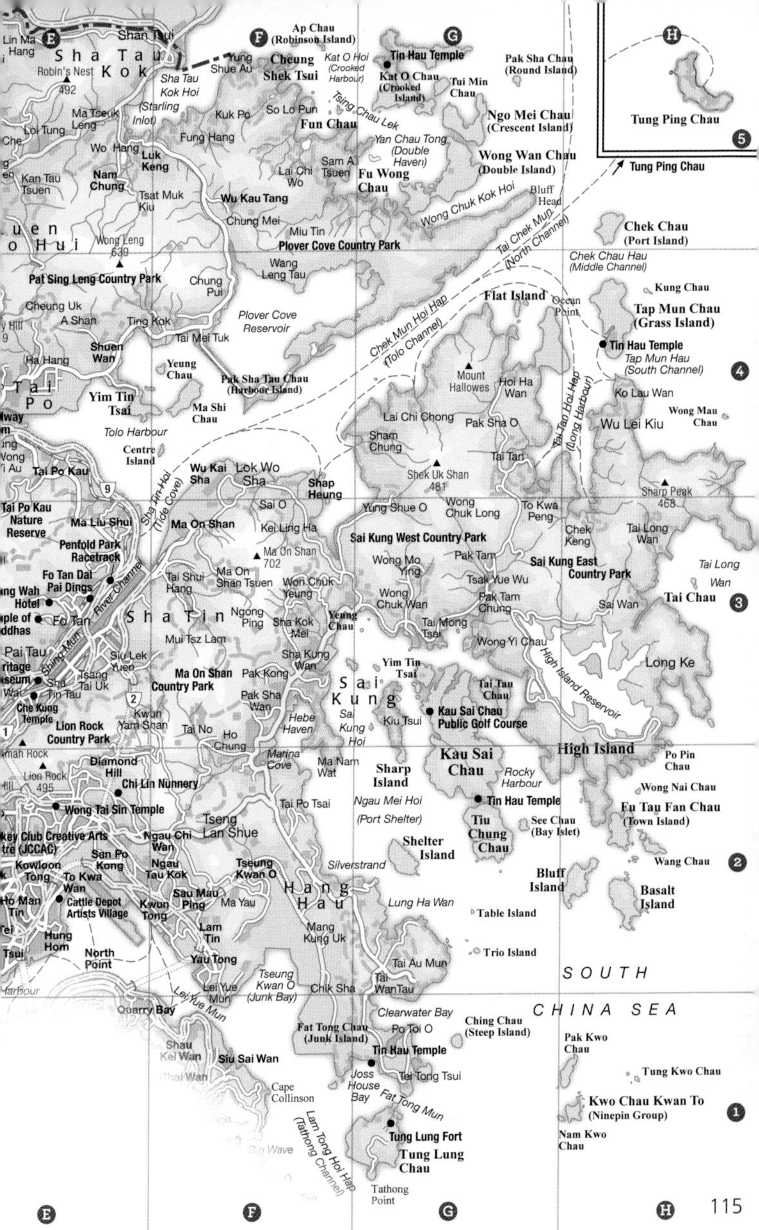

E
F
G
H
Lin Ma Hang
Sha Tau Kok
Shan Tsui
Robin's Nest
492
Sha Tau Kok Hoi
(Starling Inlet)
Yung Shue Au
Ap Chau
(Robinson Island)
Cheung Shek Tsui
Kat O Hoi
(Crooked Harbour)
Tin Hau Temple
Kat O Chau
(Crooked Island)
Tui Min Chau
Pak Sha Chau
(Round Island)
Tung Ping Chau
5
Tung Ping Chau
Ma Tseuk Leng
Loi Tung
Che
Kuk Po
So Lo Pun
Tsing Chau Lek
Fun Chau
Ngo Mei Chau
(Crescent Island)
Wo Hang
Fung Hang
Yan Chau Tong
(Double Haven)
Wong Wan Chau
(Double Island)
Luk Keng
Kan Tau Tsuen
Nam Chung
Lai Chi Wo
Sam A Tsuen
Fu Wong Chau
Tsat Muk Kiu
Wu Kau Tang
Wong Chuk Kok Hoi
Bluff Head
Chung Mei
Miu Tin
Wong Leng
639
Plover Cove Country Park
Tai Chek Mun
(North Channel)
Chek Chau
(Port Island)
Chek Chau Hau
(Middle Channel)
Pat Sing Leng Country Park
Wang Leng Tau
Chung Pui
Cheung Uk
A Shan
Ting Kok
Plover Cove Reservoir
Flat Island
Ocean Point
Kung Chau
Tap Mun Chau
(Grass Island)
Chek Mun Hoi Hap
(Tolo Channel)
Tin Hau Temple
Tap Mun Hau
(South Channel)
Tai Mei Tuk
Shuen Wan
Ha Hang
Yeung Chau
Pak Sha Tau Chau
(Harbour Island)
Mount Hallowes
Hoi Ha Wan
Tai Tan Hoi Hap
(Long Harbour)
Ko Lau Wan
4
Tai Po
Yim Tin Tsai
Ma Shi Chau
Tolo Harbour
Lai Chi Chong
Pak Sha O
Wong Mau Chau
Wu Lei Kiu
Centre Island
Sham Chung
Tai Tan
Tai Po Kau
Wu Kai Sha
Lok Wo Sha
Sha Tin Hoi
(Tide Cove)
Shap Heung
Shek Uk Shan
481
Sharp Peak
468
9
Tai Po Kau Nature Reserve
Ma Liu Shui
Ma On Shan
Sai O
Yung Shue O
Wong Chuk Long
To Kwa Peng
Kei Ling Ha
Sai Kung West Country Park
Chek Keng
Tai Long Wan
Penfold Park Racetrack
Ma On Shan
702
Wong Mo Ying
Pak Tam
Sai Kung East Country Park
Tai Long Wan
Fo Tan Dai Pai Dings
Tai Shui Hang
Ma On Shan Tsuen
Wong Chuk Yeung
Tsak Yue Wu
Sai Wan
Tai Chau
3
Shing Mun River Channel
Fo Tan
Sha Tin
Ngong Ping
Sha Kok Mei
Yeung Chau
Wong Chuk Wan
Pak Tam Chung
Tai Mong Tsai
Mui Tsz Lam
Wong Yi Chau
High Island Reservoir
Pai Tau
Siu Lek Yuen
Sha Kung Wan
Yim Tin Tsai
Long Ke
Tsang Tai Uk
Ma On Shan Country Park
Pak Kong
Sai Kung
Tai Tau Chau
Sha Tin Tau
Che Kung Temple
Pak Sha Wan
Kau Sai Chau Public Golf Course
2
Kwun Yam Shan
Hebe Haven
Sai Kung Hoi
Kiu Tsui
Lion Rock Country Park
Tai No
Ho Chung
1
Lion Rock
495
Diamond Hill
Marina Cove
Ma Nam Wat
Sharp Island
Kau Sai Chau
High Island
Po Pin Chau
Rocky Harbour
Chi Lin Nunnery
Wong Nai Chau
Wong Tai Sin Temple
Tai Po Tsai
Ngau Mei Hoi
(Port Shelter)
Tin Hau Temple
Fu Tau Fan Chau
(Town Island)
Tseng Lan Shue
Tiu Chung Chau
See Chau
(Bay Islet)
Ngau Chi Wan
Shelter Island
San Po Kong
Wang Chau
2
Kowloon Tong
To Kwa Wan
Ngau Tau Kok
Tseung Kwan O
Silverstrand
Bluff Island
Basalt Island
Cattle Depot Artists Village
Kwun Tong
Sau Mau Ping
Ma Yau
Hang Hau
Lung Ha Wan
Table Island
Hung Hom
Lam Tin
Mang Kung Uk
North Point
Yau Tong
Trio Island
Tai Au Mun
SOUTH
Lei Yue Mun
Tseung Kwan O
(Junk Bay)
Chik Sha
Tai Wan Tau
CHINA SEA
Quarry Bay
Clearwater Bay
Ching Chau
(Steep Island)
Fat Tong Chau
(Junk Island)
Po Toi O
Pak Kwo Chau
Shau Kei Wan
Siu Sai Wan
Tin Hau Temple
Tung Kwo Chau
Chai Wan
Joss House Bay
Tai Tong Tsui
Cape Collinson
Fat Tong Mun
Kwo Chau Kwan To
(Ninepin Group)
1
Lam Tong Hoi Hap
(Tathong Channel)
Tung Lung Fort
Nam Kwo Chau
Big Wave
Tung Lung Chau
Tathong Point
E
F
G
H

Swing a golf club in the midst of stunning scenery at Kau Sai Chau

MORE COURSES

Good concierges should be able to swing you a favour on greens elsewhere, but two other clubs allow visitors and can be booked independently: also in the New Territories, **Clearwater Bay Golf & Country Club** (139 Tai Au Mun Road, Clearwater Bay; tel: 2719 1595; www.cwbgolf.org) and, over on Lantau Island, **Discovery Bay Golf Club** (tel: 2987 2112; www.dbgc.hk). Both clubs are very scenic, with restaurants and everything a golfer might need to hire. Visitor access is on weekdays, though only for three days a week at Discovery Bay.

While an old-school flavour of privilege permeates most members-only golf courses, the public course at **Kau Sai Chau** is a rare down-to-earth treat. Moreover, it is beautifully landscaped, having been sculpted on part of the small, verdant island of the same name in the eastern New Territories.

Get the MTR to Choi Hung, then a taxi or no. 92 bus to Sai Kung's small harbour, where the course has its own clearly marked pier. The 20-minute boat ride there and back is a pleasant experience in itself: as the small vessel pulls out to semi-open water, Sai Kung harbour appears quite picturesque, with its fishing boats and sampans framed against a mountainous backdrop.

Kau Sai Chau has two 18-hole courses, and clubs, shoes, trolleys and caddies are all available for hire. There is also a large driving range, floodlit after twilight. Do note that out-of-town visitors can play on weekdays only – this is Hong Kong's sole public course, and is much in demand at weekends and on public holidays.

Kau Sai Chau Public Golf Course; Sai Kung; tel: 2791 3388; www.kscgolf.org.hk; daily 7am–8pm; map G3

Catch your own **squid** on a **trawler at night**

Sai Kung harbour is lined with open-fronted seafood restaurants, which are a destination in themselves for many an urban Hong Konger.

A mind-boggling array of live marine life from local and overseas waters fills bubbling display aquariums: razor clams, horseshoe crabs and giant garoupa are some of the most eye-catching. Feel free to ask what's what and how it's cooked; steaming with ginger, spring onion and soy is a signature Cantonese method, although pan-frying, deep-frying and enhancing with chilli are also popular.

Some restaurants, and tour operators across Hong Kong, offer short evening cruises where you can hook your own squid and cuttlefish, which are taken ashore at the end of the expedition to be cooked in seafront restaurant kitchens as part of a set meal. A trip offshore at night is a tranquil experience, with the reflected Sai Kung waterfront shimmering about a kilometre away. This is a seasonal activity, as squid is particularly plentiful from around May to July. Catching squid is pretty much guaranteed: they are slow-moving, and attracted to the surface by light rather than bait. A recommended trip is with **Tung Kee** restaurant (96–102 Man Nin Street; tel: 2792 7493).

Boarding a boat is a fun end to a day in this laid-back town or at the beaches that are within easy reach. From restaurant tables at night, squid trawlers and their spotlights are always visible, dotted along the horizon.

Sai Kung harbour; map F3

Escape the crowds and head to a beautiful and **tranquil beach**

While Hong Kong's Southside beaches get fairly busy at weekends and holidays, some of those in the New Territories are more off the beaten track. Given the modest effort required to reach **Clearwater Bay**, the rewards are great: its well-maintained beaches are surrounded by hills and are seriously striking. The bay is a little busier at weekends, when pleasure boats drop anchor offshore.

Catch bus no. 91 from Diamond Hill MTR station and spend some time lazing on one of two long soft-sand stretches: if you are with kids, there is plenty of space here for them to let off steam. Simply named **Clearwater Bay First Beach** and **Second Beach**, there are lifeguards, showers and barbecue areas. Food supplies are limited to a kiosk on Second Beach, which also serves cooked dishes. Your best bet is to stock up at the **Park N Shop** supermarket in Plaza Hollywood above the MTR station.

Set back in the hills overlooking the beaches is Tai Hang Tun Barbecue Area, where barbecue and picnic facilities are provided, and there are some magnificent vistas out over the open sea. A popular kite-flying area on breezy days, it is also the starting point for several hiking trails up the peaks of Clearwater Bay Country Park. An easy-going 1.5km walk cuts across dense woodlands, with 15 information boards on plantlife, and the chance to see plenty of butterflies and dragonflies.

Clearwater Bay; map G1

Gear yourself up for a demanding **hike** along the **MacLehose Trail**

Traversing the New Territories for 100km from west to east, the **MacLehose Trail** takes in the most dramatic mountain and coastal views in Hong Kong. Scrub-covered hills, occasional jutting rocky escarpments and reservoirs punctuate the western sections from Tai Lam Country Park in Tuen Mun, with one ridge after another spanning out to the eastern mangroves and sandy bays of Sai Kung Country Park, which the trail loops around to the east.

Pick up a detailed map and take on a section. In the west, 6.3km Route Twisk snakes from Tsuen Wan (map D3) to Lead Mine Pass, via Hong Kong's tallest peak, Tai Mo Shan. Its summit is often shrouded in cloud or mist – so pick a clear day for views across Kowloon and

the New Territories. The Tsuen Wan starting point is best reached by taxi from the MTR station to Tsuen Kam Au; for Lead Mine Pass, catch a cab from Tai Po KCR (Kowloon-Canton Railway) station.

In the east, Pak Tam Chung Visitor Centre (map G3) is the start of numerous walks. Further east into Sai Kung East Country Park, the trail hugs High Island Reservoir, from where paths lead to several of the territory's most unspoilt beaches – including Tai Long Wan (p.120). To reach the starting point, get a bus or minibus to Sai Kung from Diamond Hill or Choi Hung MTR stations; then get bus no. 94 bound for Wong Shek Pier, and alight at Pak Tam Chung.

Hop on a speedboat which will deliver you to a top beach and **snorkelling spot**

Reaching **Tai Long Wan** is quite a mission. From Wong Shek Pier, embark on a thrilling 15-minute speedboat ride round to Chek Keng, then join the MacLehose Trail *(p.119)* and hike for an hour over the ridge to Hong Kong's most stunning bay where you are rewarded for your efforts.

There are two long swathes of pale, powdery sand, and usually enough surf to make it worth lugging a surfboard over the hill (the name means Big Wave Bay). But it is never crowded, and the water at the shore's edge is pretty calm, thanks to the colourful coral that breaks the waves. The water also teems with vibrant fish, and you can rent snorkels to observe them. Surfboards are also for hire, as are pitched tents for those who

feel like stopping over – or bring your own. Modest restaurants and shower facilities are available.

To get to Wong Shek Pier, catch the bus from Diamond Hill or Choi Hung MTR stations to Sai Kung, then bus no. 94; or on Sundays and holidays, bus no. 96R from Diamond Hill via Sai Kung.

For even more pristine waters, head to **Hoi Ha Wan**, home to a protected marine park; two-thirds of Hong Kong's 88 hard coral species are found here, as well as a WWF starfish conservation project. Again, shops offer snorkel gear for hire. Eco-tours are given; see www.afcd.gov.hk. Get there on the no. 7 minibus from Sai Kung.

Tai Long Wan; map H3
Hoi Ha Wan; map G4

Share an evening with **Sai Kung**'s expats in its **cosy restaurants and pubs**

The eastern New Territories town of **Sai Kung** has a similarly laid-back feel to some of the territory's outlying islands, but without the need to worry about ferry timetables. This neck of the woods has long had a small, loyal non-native community, who tend to commute into town from one of the 20 or so low-rise villages dotted around it.

As well as a host of waterfront seafood restaurants, Sai Kung has a smattering of cosy Continental, Italian and other internationally flavoured bistros and bars, where you can mingle with the town's expat community and enjoy a relaxed end to a day trip around this area.

Laid-back bar-restaurant **Hebe One O One** (112 Pak Sha Wan; tel: 2335 5515) has friendly staff and regulars, and a tasty Continental menu.

For Mediterranean-influenced Australian food, long-standing **Jaspa's Restaurant** (13 Sha Tsui Path; tel: 2792 6388) draws locals back again and again. So does the casual café next door, **Ali Oli Bakery** (11 Sha Tsui Path; tel: 2792 2655).

Of Sai Kung's few pubs, **Steamers Bar** (18–32 Chan Man Street, tel: 2792 6991) is a local favourite. Serving full English breakfasts in the mornings, it switches into a lunch spot and bar in the afternoon.

Sai Kung; map F3

ONE-THIRTYONE

For a treat in the area, quality French restaurant **one-thirtyone** (131 Tseng Tau Village Road; tel: 2791 2684; www.one-thirtyone. com) is set in a converted three-storey village house on the quiet bay of Three Fathoms Cove. Surrounded by well-kept gardens, it is a great setting for a gastronomic treat or a romantic meal. The seasonal menu changes daily: expect home-made bread, and the likes of mushroom soup, pan-fried foie gras, cheeses and a trio of desserts. Advance bookings must be made.

Unleash your inner trainspotter at the **Hong Kong Railway Museum**

There are a few museums scattered around the New Territories, and the **Hong Kong Railway Museum** is perhaps the most charismatic, evoking some sense of what **Tai Po** may have been like before its full-on development as a New Town in the 1980s.

The museum's structure, with ornate upturned Chinese eaves and grey roof tiles, was formerly Tai Po Market Station; though at first glance, with its protective rooftop figurines, it might be mistaken for a traditional southern Chinese temple. It would have stood facing arable and livestock farmland when built in 1913. These days, Tai Po Market KCR station is just around the corner.

Its railway days ceased in 1983, but the renovated ticketing office and signalling room have been kept as true to the building's earliest years as possible. Other rooms display models of the evolution of both local and overseas trains. Real vintage locomotives and carriages in pristine condition can be inspected and boarded in the grounds – kids love them.

Another excellent museum in the New Territories is the **Hong Kong Heritage Museum** in Sha Tin, which contains a highly interactive mix of exhibits on history, art and culture – with specific focus on Hong Kong and Southern China. Little ones will enjoy the Children's Discovery Gallery. Six thematic galleries host regularly changing vibrant exhibitions, showcasing different corners of the territory and its environs, and explaining local traditions. The museum is signposted from Che Kung Temple KCR station.

Hong Kong Railway Museum; 13 Shung Tak Street, Tai Po Market; tel: 2653 3455; Wed–Mon 9am–5pm; free; map E4
Hong Kong Heritage Museum; 1 Man Lam Road, Sha Tin; tel: 2180 8188; www. heritagemuseum.gov.hk; Wed–Mon 10am–6pm, Sun and public hols till 7pm; charge, Wed free; map E3

Take a **leisurely bike-ride** along **Tai Mei Tuk**'s lakeside cycle paths

Tai Po and its environs are a great place to head for some pedalling. Get there on the KCR, rent a bike from shops around Tai Po Market and embark on a 10km trip skirting the bases of Pat Sing Leng Country Park's sizeable mountains, northeast to **Tai Mei Tuk**. Here you can explore **Plover Cove Country Park**, with some of Hong Kong's finest natural scenery. For a more leisurely ride, get bus no. 75K from Tai Po Market to Tai Mei Tuk and rent a bike there.

Beautiful Plover Cove Reservoir was completed in 1968. A dam was built into the sea, with the resulting lake drained of seawater and filled with freshwater from newly created hillside channels. Today, you can cycle or walk between this fresh body on one side and the sea on the other. Heading north with the reservoir on your right, a beautiful path takes you through woodland rapids to Bride's Pool and Mirror Pool, each with plunging waterfalls.

Also in the vicinity is **Tai Po Kau Nature Reserve**, worth considering for serious hikers – a thick forest on a steep hillside. Get there on minibus no. 28K from Tai Po Market, bound for Sha Tin.

Tai Po; map E4
Plover Cove Reservoir; map F4
Tai Po Kau Nature Reserve; map E3

Combine dinner at the acclaimed **Sha Tin 18** restaurant with a **trip to the races**

A few restaurants in Hong Kong offer quality menus that represent the cuisines of more than one region of China, and **Sha Tin 18** is a splendid example.

Its top regional Chinese chefs man separate kitchen stations in an open dining room at the Hyatt Regency hotel in Sha Tin. Northern Chinese and Cantonese cuisine is meticulously prepared. There's always something dynamic to watch, whether handmade noodles being stretched and cut or large woks frying, steaming and boiling. The Peking duck is a highlight, carved tableside and served as three courses: with

pancakes; then chopped and stir-fried; and finally as a light broth.

Come on a Sunday and combine it with a day at the horse races, held every weekend at **Penfold Park Racetrack** except in the sultry summer months. You must be over 18 years of age and hold a valid passport. For a splurge, buy a Tourist Badge at the members' main entrance, which lets you take box seats, roam the members' betting halls and trackside areas and dine and drink at members-only outlets. The public stands offer an earthier experience, and the world's longest high-definition Diamond Vision television screen makes sure you catch every detail.

There are more food outlets to choose from at **New Town Plaza** mall, from noodle houses and cafés to vegetarian cuisine and Japanese restaurants. This complex also has some of the best shops on offer in the New Territories and a cinema.

Sha Tin 18; Hyatt Regency Hong Kong, 18 Chak Cheung Street; tel: 3723 1234; map E3
Penfold Park Racetrack, Sha Tin; tel: 1817; www.hkjc.com; Sun, sometimes Wed and Sat 10am–6pm, races start after midday; charge; map E3
New Town Plaza; Sha Tin Centre Street; www.newtownplaza.com.hk; map E3

Improve your lot with a spin on the **wheel of fortune** or marvel at more than **10,000 Buddhas**

Few modern cities take their traditional beliefs as seriously as Hong Kong, and the New Territories provide some good opportunities for you to get a temple fix.

Che Kung Temple is dedicated to Taoist deity General Che Kung, who quashed a rebellion in South China during the Sung dynasty (960–1279), and accompanied the Emperor when he fled to Hong Kong. After his death, people began worshipping him for his courage. The temple grounds feature a huge, ancient drum and bell. But most noteworthy is a copper fan-bladed wheel of fortune, which is believed to bring good luck when turned three times. Fortune-tellers can be found near the entrance.

A visit here is particularly enjoyable during the first three days of the Lunar New Year festival (its date varies yearly from January to February), when the atmosphere is pretty animated, with local residents praying for good fortune in the year ahead or giving thanks for help in the previous one.

One of the most impressive temples in Hong Kong is in the New Territories: the **Temple of 10,000 Buddhas** (*pictured*). There are actually more than 10,000 miniature Buddha images here, but in Cantonese tradition this number implies an inconceivably large amount. A visit to the temple provides some built-in exercise: the 431-step climb to reach it. The entrance is guarded by a variety of fearsome protectors, and inside a striking selection of gold Buddhas lines the walls. Elsewhere in the grounds is a nine-storey pagoda.

Che Kung Temple; Tai Wai; tel: 2603 4049; daily 7am–6pm; free; map E3
Temple of 10,000 Buddhas; Sha Tin; tel: 2691 1067; daily 9am–5pm; free; map E3

Enjoy **roast pigeon** in Fo Tan or Sha Tin

For the authentic food fan, there are two reasons to head up to the **Fo Tan** or **Sha Tin** areas of the New Territories. The first is to eat roast pigeon, a speciality dish, though not exclusive to these parts. The second is to experience a *dai pai dong*. These no-nonsense restaurants, with outdoor kitchens and tables, used to dot local streets, and many a favourite earthy Hong Kong dish was best enjoyed at one. But city authorities deemed them potential health hazards, and most have been moved off the pavement into soulless 'cooked food' areas of government-run indoor markets. As with similarly almost-extinct street snack stalls, new licences have not been granted for new vendors for around a decade.

Luckily, Fo Tan has a number of *dai pai dongs*, serving up the robust likes of fried noodles and clay-pot rice right next to the KCR station. But the pigeon is a must-try: the meat is dark, lean and pleasantly flavoured – much like the dark meat of chicken – and the skin is crisp. It comes with two dips – one a honey-based sauce, the other spiced salt. Enjoy with rice and vegetable or bean curd dishes, and a bottle of Tsing Tao beer or tea. Take your pick from the *dai pai dongs*, though **Chun** **Chun** is the largest and serves consistently top-notch fowl.

A more upmarket pigeon tasting can be had at another foodie institution: **Lung Wah Hotel**, situated on the hills of Sha Tin. Despite its name, this restaurant ceased hostelry operations decades ago, and is certainly off the beaten track, requiring a short taxi hop from town to get there.

Chun Chun; Fo Tan KCR station; tel: 2691 2660; map E3
Lung Wah Hotel; 22 Ha Wo Che, Sha Tin; tel: 2691 1594; www.lungwahhotel.hk; map E3

Decide whether a 12-metre **granite pillar** looks like **a mother and baby**

Perched above what is now the Sha Tin end of the Lion Rock Tunnel from Kowloon, **Amah Rock** is so named as it is believed to resemble an *amah*, or nanny, carrying a baby in a sling on her back. One myth supposes that the form was actually a real woman, turned to stone by Tin Hau, Goddess of the Sea, after her fisherman husband failed to return from an expedition out on the open water. Another version claims the woman became petrified in stone as she waited, motionless, for her missing husband to return.

The rock has become deified as a shrine to women and fertility and a symbol of female loyalty and fidelity. Women who have conceived a child after coming here, and making an offering of fruit and/or incense, regularly return to give thanks. Others say its powers of fertility lie in its phallic rather than figurative form.

Get the KCR to Tai Wai station, then bus no. 81C, 86A, 86B, 86C, 87A or 89B to Hung Miu Kuk Road and follow the signs to the rock. Make the medium-level but steep hike up the hill, examine the 15-metre tall pillar of weathered granite, and see whether the romantic legends can triumph over your 21st-century pragmatism.

The views of Sha Tin across rolling hills are impressive, and it is worth timing the ascent for late afternoon on a clear day, which allows for an even finer panorama over Kowloon and the New Territories.

Amah Rock; map E3

Cross a small moat to one of Hong Kong's last
fortress communities

The Walled Villages of the New Territories trace their roots to the 10th century, when the 'five clans' built these fortified settlements to protect themselves from marauding outsiders, and each other. Later villages were occupied by the *Hakka*, Chinese migrants who moved here in the 17th to 18th centuries and lived apart from the Cantonese. The way of life in the walled villages remains fairly traditional, so it is worth paying the small donation to enter. The price for taking a picture of a *Hakka* woman wearing a traditional fringed hat will vary.

The most popular for visitors is the **Kat Hing Wai** village – to get there, take the KCR to Kam Sheung Road Station. Some 400 people live there, and most of them still share the same surname, Tang. Built in the 1600s, the fortified village shelters behind walls 6 metres thick, with guard-houses at each corner, arrow slits for fighting off attackers, and a moat. There is still just one entrance, guarded by a heavy wrought-iron gate.

Over in Tsuen Wan, the **Sam Tung Uk Museum** was lived in by the Chan clan until they vacated the site in the 1980s and the government reconstructed it as a museum. Inside are rows of traditional houses and four original dwellings erected in 1786. There is also an ancestral memorial hall.

Kat Hing Wai Village; map C4
Sam Tung Uk Museum; Kwu Uk Lane, Tsuen Wan; tel: 2411 2001; Wed-Mon 9am–5pm; free; map D3

Embark on a guided tour of **Kadoorie Farm** animal conservation centre

Located to the west of Tai Po, **Kadoorie Farm & Botanic Garden** is about as far from urban Hong Kong as it is possible to get. Set up by the immigrant Kadoorie family in the 1950s to help local farmers, it has since evolved into a conservation centre and a pioneer of organic farming in Hong Kong.

More than half of Hong Kong's plant species grow here, and on the farm, pigs, cows and fowl are all kept and bred. Conservation projects include the rehabilitation of reptiles and birds of prey, and research enclosures include waterfowl, deer and butterflies. Make your own way there via Tai Po Market KCR and the no. 64K bus, or join a tour through local travel agents. Organic fresh and dry produce is also sold here.

Northwest of Kadoorie, occupying some of the last of the territory's wetland, are two other ecological zones: **Mai Po Marshes** and **Hong Kong Wetland Park**. Mai Po's 380-hectare marshes are the temporary home to rare migratory birds; WWF Hong Kong runs tours, as do some local travel agents. The 61-hectare Wetland Park, in Tin Shui Wai, is a world-class conservation site where you might spot egrets, kingfishers and black-faced spoonbills. Get the

MTR to Tin Shui Wai, then Light Rail 705 to Wetland Park Station.

Kadoorie Farm & Botanic Garden; Lam Kam Road, Tai Po; tel: 2488 1317; www.kfbg.org.hk; daily 9.30am–5pm, by appointment only; free; map D4
Mai Po Marshes; Lok Ma Chau; visit through WWF Hong Kong; tel: 2526 1011; www.wwf.org.hk; charge; map C4/5
Hong Kong Wetland Park; Tin Shui Wai; tel: 3152 2666; www.wetlandpark. com; charge; map B4

Seek calm at Tsuen Wan's temples and monasteries

Off Tsuen Wan's **Lo Wai Road**, which leads to some of Hong Kong's less touristy monastery complexes, lies a quiet surprise.

Visible down a short shrub-covered slope, the white prow of a ship points its way forward along a boulder-strewn stream. At its prow, where a captain might stand, is a colourful upright statue of Kwan Kung, a fierce deity favoured by police, armed forces and even triads. At the stern is a serene white statue of Guan Yin, Goddess of Mercy; around her, plumes of smoke curl upwards at a red altar.

This may sound like a conceptual artwork lying in the landlocked northwest New Territories hills, but it is actually a living temple and shrine. On closer inspection, the whole 'vessel' is made of whitewashed concrete, and can be boarded by steps from a path. It has no official name, but characters on its side read Heung Hoi Tse Hong Boat Temple.

Head uphill for 100 metres or so and on the opposite side of the same road is the **Yuen Yuen Institute**, a string of ornate structures that house a slew of Buddhist and Taoist deities and protectors. Its fishpond- and pagoda-punctuated grounds are also home to a Confucian temple.

The arches of all three religions are erected at the entrance of the institute, which was built in the 1950s. The main building of the institute, called the Great Temple of the Three Religions, is modelled on the architecture of the Temple of Heaven in Beijing, and in this temple deities of the three belief systems are enshrined. The complex is usually tranquil on weekdays, but weekends and public holidays are more bustling.

On any day, it is possible to hear the low-toned daily prayers of resident monks, or the meandering percussion-accompanied horn harmonies played

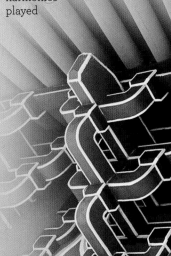

live as paper offerings are burnt in memory of the deceased. A vegetarian meal can be had here between 9am and 5pm. Get there via Tsuen Wan MTR station and minibus no. 81 from Shiu Wo to Yuen Yuen Institute.

A 2km walk west to Chuk Lam Sim (or by minibus 85 if coming from Tsuen Wan MTR Station, Exit B1), on Fu Yung Shan hill lies the small Buddhist **Chuk Lam Sim Monastery** (*pictured*), meaning Bamboo Forest Monastery. Built over a period of five decades from 1932, the monastery has a gallery of ink paintings and calligraphy by celebrated South China artists. Fringed by foothills, the tiered landscaping is lush, and well-spaced whitewashed monastic buildings are connected by raised footpaths. Buddha statues in the main temple hall are some of the largest on display in Hong Kong.

Heung Hoi Tse Hong Boat Temple; 33 Lo Wai Road, Sam Dip Tam; map D3
Yuen Yuen Institute; Lo Wai Road; tel: 2492 2220; daily 8.30am–5.30pm; map D3
Chuk Lam Sim Monastery; Fu Yung Shan Road; tel: 2416 6557; daily 7.30am–5.30pm; map D3

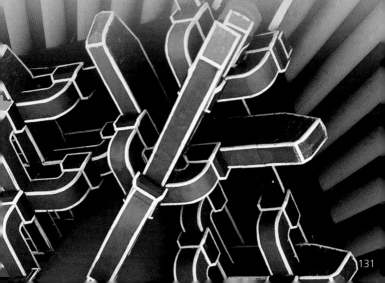

Saddle up on an **ex-racehorse** and trot in a
grassy paddock surrounded by lychee trees

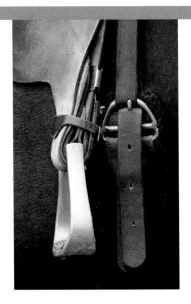

or with a companion on a
different horse. Lessons, which
are available in English and
Cantonese, specialise in dressage,
showjumping and cross-country
training, and all skill levels are
catered for. There is both a grass
paddock and an arena with
sawdust-strewn flooring.

There are two other operations
over on Hong Kong Island. Many
of the animals at the three riding
schools are retired racehorses
that have undergone retraining
programmes.

*Tuen Mun Public Riding School; Lot 45
Lung Mun Road; tel: 2461 3338; www.
hkjc.com; map B3*

The Hong Kong Jockey Club, the
not-for-profit organisation that
runs the two racetracks and all
off-site bookmaking and lottery
sales in the territory, ploughs its
revenue back into community
projects. It operates three horse-
riding schools that are open to
the public, and by far the most
scenically situated is **Tuen Mun
Public Riding School**.

The facility is in an idyllic
spot, surrounded by grass and
greenery that includes old lychee
trees. Visitors can arrange to
ride with individual instruction

KAYAK CAPER

For a more thrilling workout while
still appreciating the great outdoors,
kayak around some of the New
Territories' mangrove-lined, rocky
and sandy coastlines. **Kayak and
Hike** (tel: 9300 5197; www.kayak-
and-hike.com) offers tailor-made
packages, including paddling straight
off the shore and power-boating
to areas of geological interest.
Alternatively, check out the **Tai Mei
Tuk Watersport Centre** (Plover Cove
Reservoir, Tai Po; tel: 2665 3591;
map F4) and other government-run
venues (www.lcsd.gov.hk/watersport)
that hire out kayaks and run courses
and expeditions.

Gaze across the **shimmering marina** at **Gold Coast**

Next to Castle Peak Bay in the northwest New Territories is the Mediterranean-themed resort complex called **Hong Kong Gold Coast**. European-inspired architecture dots Golden Beach, Hong Kong's first man-made beach, which stretches for more than half a kilometre. From the beach, a promenade leads to Dolphin Square, where it is often possible to spot rare local pink dolphins offshore.

The resort offers a different flavour to the everyday city bustle. Take your pick from a dozen or so restaurants at **Gold Coast Piazza**. All are open-fronted or -sided and overlook the bay and marina; the atmosphere is pretty laid back.

Chilli N Spice Seafood Market (Shop 26, G/F; tel: 2430 1166) is popular with resident expats and Chinese; the fiery menu features Southeast Asian curries and chilli-enhanced regional dishes. **Sun Wing Restaurant** (Shop 29, G/F; tel: 2440 8080) serves up a wide range of Cantonese favourites.

At the **Yacht and Country Club** (tel: 2404 3257), yachts or motorised pleasure boats can be chartered and fishing trips arranged. To soak up the atmosphere at leisure, consider a stay at the five-star **Hong Kong Gold Coast Hotel** (p.178).

Hong Kong Gold Coast; 1 Castle Peak Road, Castle Peak Bay; www.goldcoast. com.hk; map B3

Marvel at the unique **geology** of **Tung Ping Chau**

Though really an 'outer island', **Tung Ping Chau** is one of two in the far-flung northeast of Hong Kong that doesn't have a ferry connection from Central, as this would be much too long a journey. In fact, lying some distance east of Mirs Bay, it's usually off the main maps and is just 3km off the Guangdong coast. From its hilltops, you get a panoramic view of the mainland's Bao An area.

Once supporting a population of close to 3,000, today Ping Chau is almost unpopulated, most islanders having moved to urban areas or emigrated years ago. The 2km-long, mostly flat island, officially part of Plover Cove Country Park, is made of what are known as 'thousand-layer rocks' (comprising layered siltstone and chert) in different shapes and colours. There are other natural attractions as well, including caves and waterfalls, plus old-fashioned stone houses with courtyards and winding passages.

Coral heads lie just off a pristine sandy beach; the waters are bluer here than anywhere in Hong Kong and snorkels can be rented. Tai Tong Village has small restaurants and shops, and offers snorkelling and diving trips and simple accommodation.

A 90-minute ferry connection run by **Tsui Wah Ferry Service** (tel: 2272 2000; www.traway.com. hk) is available on weekends and public holidays. From Sha Tin KCR Station, get the minibus to Ma Liu Shui ferry pier – ferries leave at 9am; return ferry from Tung Ping Chau is at 3.30pm.

Tung Ping Chau; map H5

Pack your tent and take a picnic to **Grass Island**

Also known as Tap Mun Chau, **Grass Island** is the second sparsely inhabited northeast New Territories outlying island. Closer to the shore than Tung Ping Chau (*p.134*), the journey itself is a pleasant 30-minute ride on a small ferry from Wong Shek Pier in Sai Kung Country Park. Make a short hop over for a breath of fresh air.

If you want to use the island's campsite, tents can be bought in Sai Kung Town at shops that sell outdoor supplies. Stock up there too on picnic supplies – there are supermarkets, bakeries and health-food shops – before catching bus no. 94 to Wong Shek Pier. Contact **Tsui Wah Ferry Service** for timetables (tel: 2272 2000; www.traway.com.hk).

Despite its dwindling fisher-folk population, the rugged island is still home to three small temples. Two, unsurprisingly, are dedicated to Goddess of the Sea, Tin Hau; the other to Goddess of Mercy, Guan Yin. The Tin Hau temples are pristinely maintained structures, originally built in the 18th century.

But it's the natural beauty and slow-paced rural life that are most striking here. Paths lead up to its central rolling grassy hills, the domain of grazing cattle – an unusual scene in Hong Kong. The campsite is up here too, and signposted.

The island's eastern shore has a jagged rocky coast, with pebbles and some sand on the western side. Back at the fishing village, small boats ply the waters daily and dried shrimp and squid can be bought from fishermen.

Grass Island; map H4

Southside

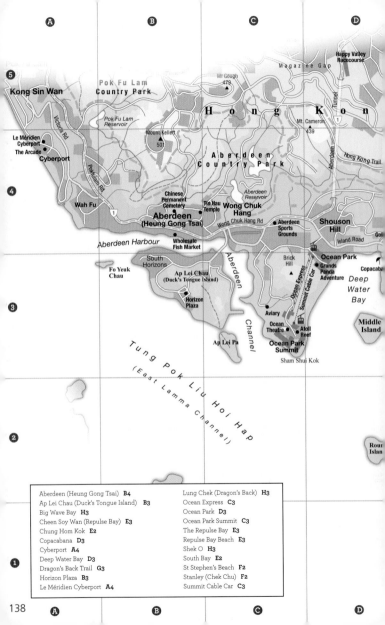

A
B
C
D

⑤ Kong Sin Wan
Pok Fu Lam Country Park
Mt Gough 479
Magazine Gap
Happy Valley Racecourse

H o n g K o n

Pok Fu Lam Reservoir
Mount Kellett 501
Mt. Cameron 439

Le Méridien Cyberport
The Arcade
Cyberport

Aberdeen Country Park

Aberdeen Trail

④ Wah Fu
Victoria Rd
Pok Fu Lam Rd

Chinese Permanent Cemetery
Tin Hau Temple
Wong Chuk Hang
Aberdeen Reservoir
Wong Chuk Hang Rd
Aberdeen Sports Grounds
Shouson Hill
Aberdeen (Heung Gong Tsai)
Island Road
Gol

Aberdeen Harbour
Wholesale Fish Market

Brick Hill
Ocean Express
Ocean Park
Grands Panda Adventure
Copacabana
Deep Water Bay

Fo Yeuk Chau
South Horizons
Ap Lei Chau (Duck's Tongue Island)

③
Horizon Plaza

Aberdeen Channel
Summit Cable Car

Aviary
Ocean Theatre
Atoll Reef
Ocean Park Summit
Middle Island

Ap Lei Pa
Sham Shui Kok

T u n g P o k L i u H o i H a p
(East Lamma Channel)

②
Rour Islan

①

Aberdeen (Heung Gong Tsai) **B4**	Lung Chek (Dragon's Back) **H3**
Ap Lei Chau (Duck's Tongue Island) **B3**	Ocean Express **C3**
Big Wave Bay **H3**	Ocean Park **D3**
Cheen Soy Wan (Repulse Bay) **E3**	Ocean Park Summit **C3**
Chung Hom Kok **E2**	The Repulse Bay **E3**
Copacabana **D3**	Repulse Bay Beach **E3**
Cyberport **A4**	Shek O **H3**
Deep Water Bay **D3**	South Bay **E2**
Dragon's Back Trail **G3**	St Stephen's Beach **F2**
Horizon Plaza **B3**	Stanley (Chek Chu) **F2**
Le Méridien Cyberport **A4**	Summit Cable Car **C3**

A
B
C
D

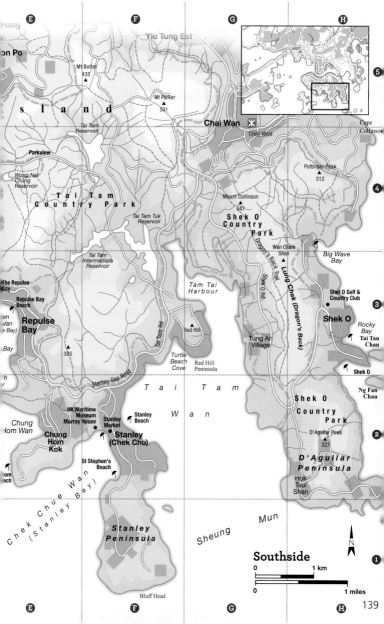

Whizz across the waves at Stanley, Deep Water Bay and Repulse Bay

In Southside you can skim the water's surface against a backdrop of golden sand, aquamarine sea and a sprinkling of rocky islands. Try water-skiing, wakeboarding or jet-skiing at **Stanley**, where there are two aqua sport centres, or a little further north at **Deep Water Bay** and adjacent **Repulse Bay**.

Stanley's two government-funded operations – **Main Beach Water Sports Centre** (tel: 2813 9117) and **St Stephen's Beach Water Sports Centre** (tel: 2813 5407) – are hugely popular. The former faces Tai Tam Bay, whose relatively calm sea conditions in summer make it an ideal place for novices to acquire the basic skills; the latter's choppier waters year-round make it more of a challenge. You can wakeboard or water-ski at Deep Water and Repulse Bay with water-sport operators such as **SeaDynamics** (tel: 2604 4747; www.seadynamics.com). Serious water-skiers should contact the **Hong Kong Water Ski Association** (tel: 2504 8168; www.waterski.org.hk).

You'll notice gated low-rise and sparkling high-rise blocks set back off Deep Water and Repulse Bays. These fetch staggering prices, with residents either from Hong Kong's most moneyed families or lucky expat contract workers.

Bus nos. 6, 6A and 260 from Exchange Square bus station in Central all serve Stanley, Deep Water and Repulse Bays.

Stanley; map F2
Deep Water Bay; map D3
Repulse Bay; map E3

Be elegantly urbane by day or night at **Repulse Bay**

Across the road from the beach, on the site of the grand Repulse Bay Hotel, demolished in the 1980s, are the faux colonial walls of **The Repulse Bay complex**. The plush restaurants, spa and shops within hint at the elite splendour that once reigned here. Today, the most popular of Hong Kong Island's beaches has certainly lost all its airs and graces, but behind this replica facade you can still find a stylish air-conditioned getaway.

Two standout restaurants are **The Verandah** (tel: 2292 2822), where Continental fine dining takes place under tall ceilings and whirling fans; and **Spices** (tel: 2292 2821), which serves a pan-Asian menu both indoors and in its small garden. There is also a tastefully decked-out café and a quality supermarket, catering primarily to the residents of adjoining and nearby luxury flats.

Scattered throughout the complex are historic photos and artefacts that recall the hotel era, when this was the place for weekend escapes from downtown Hong Kong. Among its illustrious guests were Spain's Prince Juan Carlos, Marlon Brando, George Bernard Shaw and Noël Coward.

Get a more Mediterranean experience right on the sand of Deep Water Bay at wooden-decked open-sided restaurant and lounge bar **Cococabana**. Its owner and chef hail from southern France and it's a fine spot for sundowners.

The Repulse Bay; 109 Repulse Bay Road: www.therepulsebay.com; map E3 Cococabana; 2/F, Beach Building, Deep Water Bay; tel: 2812 2226; www. toptables.com.hk; map D3

See the last of the **floating fisher-folk** families in Hong Kong

Bays and small harbours with jetties across Hong Kong were once home to thousands of boat dwellers. In Aberdeen, although there was a large-scale government programme to rehouse floating residents in flats in the same area, some families still remain in these moored wooden vessels.

From the promenade at Aberdeen Typhoon Shelter, you can see their houseboats at **Aberdeen Harbour**, moored next to each other in neat rows. For a closer look, you can charter a small wooden sampan – negotiate a reasonable sum (HK$60–80 for 20 minutes is about right) with the old ladies wearing wide-brimmed straw hats who beckon you on board. Weave between the remaining houseboats, which are often home to three generations of one family, a pet watchdog or two and even makeshift gardens of potted plants. Around 30 to 45 minutes will take you further around the harbour; if you have more time, you could request a one-way ride to nearby Sok Kwu Wan (40 minutes) or Yung Shue Wan on Lamma Island (one hour).

Back along the waterfront, some fisher-folk display and sell their dried seafood. There is also the small, dimly lit grey-brick **Tin Hau temple**, which dates from the mid-19th century. As Tin Hau is the Goddess of the Sea and protector of those who sail on it, you can be sure that there will always be sticks and coils of incense burning here.

Leave the water's edge, cross the road and have lunch or dinner in the down-to-earth town, with its well-frequented fresh produce market and traditional medicine shops. **The Aberdeen Centre** (6–12 Nam Ning Street) is home to some decent eateries. For a Cantonese rice-based meal, try **Tai Hing** (Shop A, Phase 5; tel: 2552 9820), which specialises in roast pork and goose and has great, nutritious daily soups; or for dim sum and a full Cantonese repertoire, try **Hsin Kwong Restaurant** (2/F, Phase 3; tel: 2555 0388).

There is no MTR station, but bus nos. 70 or 75 from Exchange Square bus station in Central go to Aberdeen.

Aberdeen; map B4

FLOATING FOOD AND DRINK
With its interior decked out in as much fortuitous red and gold as possible, **Jumbo Kingdom** (Shum Wan Pier Drive, Wong Chuk Hang, Aberdeen; tel: 2553 9111; www.jumbo.com.hk) is best-known as Hong Kong's famous floating restaurant – but don't overlook its top-notch Cantonese fare.

From its own jetty in the middle of the Aberdeen Typhoon Shelter promenade, jump aboard the regular shuttle to the restaurant and enjoy its signature seafood dishes that include sautéed fresh crab with chilli and garlic, and flambéed rice-wine-marinated prawns.

On the roof of its two storeys is chilled-out Western restaurant and bar **Top Deck** (tel: 2552 3331; www.cafedecogroup.com). The polished wooden flooring is strewn with low-slung armchairs, sofas and beanbags at the tables. It serves up a satisfying weekend brunch, or is a great place for a drink with panoramic views across the harbour sampans and luxury cruisers.

Hop on a bus to a **converted warehouse** block crammed with shops offering **bargains galore**

You wouldn't really guess **Ap Lei Chau** is a small islet, just offshore from Hong Kong Island, as it's linked by a flyover that joins it high above ground level. The main reason to detour over here (on bus no. 91 from Central or 92 from Causeway Bay) is to visit **Horizon Plaza**, a former warehouse packed to the gunnels with wholesale furniture stores, many specialising in Asian pieces both antique and reproduction, and a handful of designer fashion discount stores. You can bag fair-priced fabrics and home accessories, and even fine art, wine and foodstuffs.

Tequila Kola (1/F; tel: 2877 3295; www.tequilakola.com) was one of the pioneers. Its outdoor hardwood furniture, cushions, tablecloths and dining wear are contemporary with Asian accents. Chock-full of reproduction and real antique and traditional Asian furniture, rugs, homeware and accessories, sprawling **Shambala Furniture Warehouse** (2/F; tel: 2555 2997; www.shambala.com.hk) also has a small café.

For designer threads from last season, head to Horizon's outpost of one of the city's favourite department stores: **Lane Crawford Warehouse** (25/F; tel: 2118 3403) stocks several international designer brands. There are many more labels on the building's upper floors.

Horizon Plaza; 2 Lee Wing Street, Ap Lei Chau; map B3

Dine within sight of a **wide sandy beach** at **Shek O**

After a pleasant day spent being a beach bum on a lovely stretch of fine sand, you can enjoy an equally laid-back evening at sleepy Shek O's Chinese, Asian and Western-style restaurants and pubs.

Many of Hong Kong's neighbourhood restaurants double as bars – especially when the venue is open to the elements at its front or sides. One such place is local favourite **Chinese & Thai** (no. 303; tel: 2809 4426), which serves as many large bottles of beer to its tables as it does food.

As you'd expect from the name, there's an even split between its two cuisines. Fresh crunchy spring rolls and 'mixed fried rice' are popular, as are Thai chicken wrapped in *pandan* leaf, shrimp cakes, fish cakes and shrimp *tom yum coup*. This unpretentious menu hits the spot.

A drink at one of Hong Kong Island's few cult pubs, the **Black Sheep** (no. 330; tel: 2809 2021), is recommended. The cosy, relaxed watering hole also has a reasonable European menu that is a notch above pub grub standard – pizzas and roasts are often served.

Most upmarket is Cantonese **Reminisces** (no. 824; tel: 2809 2112), with a few outdoor tables and more indoors – roast goose and roast suckling pig are among its house specialities.

The fastest way to reach Shek O is to get the MTR to Shau Kei Wan station, then take bus no. 9 which terminates there. On Sundays and public holidays you can also take bus no. 309 from Central.

Shek O; map H3

Sail back in time at the **Maritime Museum**

With its 18th-century Chinese archery bows, pirate tales and hands-on exhibits that include the bridge of a container ship and a navigation simulator and radio room complete with dials, gadgets and sound effects, the waterfront **Hong Kong Maritime Museum** in the little Southside town of Stanley is one of Hong Kong's most child-friendly museums.

It traces centuries of Hong Kong's seafaring history, in Ancient and Modern galleries. It also has a striking location: the colonial arcades of **Murray House**, built as a British Army officers' mess in 1848. It originally stood in Central (on the site now occupied

by the Bank of China), but in 1982 was dismantled stone by stone and put into storage. It was reassembled in Stanley in 2001.

Murray House is also home to a handful of international restaurants and bars. Styled on colonial Vietnam, **Saigon** (Shop 101, 1/F; tel: 2899 0999), with whirling rattan ceiling fans and grand French doors that frame South China Sea views, serves up rice flour rolls, piquant salads and delicious curries. There are also some appealing open-fronted places overlooking Stanley Bay, on Stanley Market Road. Newcomer **Rocksalt** (no. 25; tel: 2899 0818) has a modern Australian menu.

A relaxed day in Stanley can also include a sandy stroll and a swim at St Stephen's Beach (p.140).

Hong Kong Maritime Museum; Murray House, Stanley Plaza; tel: 2813 2322; Tue–Sun 10am–6pm; charge; map F2

STANLEY MARKET
Also worth a look is **Stanley Market** (*pictured;* Stanley Village Road; daily 11am–6pm), with overruns of casual brands as well as winter and ski wear. The market is also a handy souvenir stop, with Chinese artwork, silk collectables, ornaments, carved stone seals and the like on offer.

Drop in on Southside's quieter, **less-visited beaches**

If the weather's good and the water's clear, Hong Kong's beaches are superb places to hang out. Not far from Hong Kong Island's favourite sandy stretches at Deep Water Bay and Repulse Bay (*p.140*), **South Bay** and **Chung Hom Kok** are noticeably quieter and offer a more chilled out beach experience. Both are sandy, and have lifeguards, changing rooms, showers, food kiosks and barbecue areas. Like all government-maintained beaches,

they have roped-off swimming areas which are under watch by lifeguards as well as a netted boundary that keeps out sharks and a certain amount of flotsam too. There are offshore rafts to swim out to.

Set back from the main road with its traffic noise and dangers, both South Bay and Chung Hom Kok are popular with families – the latter particularly so, as it also has a decent beach playground and excellent views towards Stanley Bay (this is the place to be at sunset). Chung Hom Kok is also popular with Hong Kong's gay community. There is a small ruined fortress just to the south.

On Sunday afternoons and evenings, the **South Bay Beach Club** (tel: 2812 6015; www.greenflashgroup.com.hk) serves up cocktails and a Mediterranean menu, while a DJ spins laid-back tunes.

Buses do not run directly to either beach, so get a taxi or come via nearby Repulse Bay. Note that lifeguard services are suspended from November until March.

South Bay Beach; South Bay Road, Repulse Bay; map E2
Chung Hom Kok Beach; Chung Hom Kok Road; map E2

Take a hike along the **Dragon's Back**, culminating in a well-earned **seaside meal or drink**

Spend a rewarding couple of hours undertaking one of Hong Kong's most manageable hikes, which takes you across ridges with spectacular South China views. Part of the snaking Hong Kong Trail, this walk goes from urban Chai Wan to Big Wave Bay, a few minutes from Shek O and its handful of restaurants.

Catch the MTR to the eastern end of the Island Line, **Chai Wan**. Take exit A and head for signposted Cape Collinson Cemetery; take the steps that lead right up through the cemetery, which is on a hill. At the top of the hill, trail directions are signposted – head for Shek O. The walk ascends quickly, leaving the hum of the Hong Kong streets behind. Once you're up on the first grassy ridge, several more undulate ahead, giving the Dragon's Back its name.

The walk along the dirt path, through scrub-covered terrain, is fairly gentle. As you reach sight of Shek O village and bay and descend the path, you are likely to encounter remote-control aeroplane and kite fliers, as well as the occasional paraglider.

The walk ends at **Big Wave Bay**, where a kiosk sells drinks and snacks and you can watch one of Hong Kong's few surf beaches in action. A 10-minute walk along the road leading away from the beach are Shek O's restaurants and bars and buses back to Shau Kei Wan or Central (*p.145*).

Dragon's Back; map G3

148

Come face to face with a **rare red panda** at **Ocean Park**

One of Southeast Asia's largest aquariums and theme parks and one of Hong Kong's oldest and best family attractions, **Ocean Park** has lost none of its appeal, due partly to its remarkable ability to reinvent itself. Since Hong Kong Disneyland (*p.158*) arrived in 2005, Ocean Park has stepped up its game with great results.

Relative newcomers to the park are its adorable pair of red pandas. At first glance, these ginger-furred creatures with white markings look very much like foxes, right down to the pointed snout, black whiskers and pointed ears; but their bushy tails are white with brown stripes. Check out the park's pair of giant pandas, too. In the same enclosure there is also a giant Chinese salamander – a bizarre, prehistoric-looking amphibious creature.

As well as some enormous, walk-around aquariums filled with stingrays, sharks, swordfish and turtles, you can catch shows starring trained sea lions and dolphins. All the wildlife and marine life in this park is humanely kept – with information boards constantly highlighting the fragility of the animals' natural environment.

Ocean Park also doubles as an amusement park, with two areas linked by your choice of either a scenic cable-car ride or the recently launched Ocean Express train, which simulates an underwater journey with porthole windows and LED display screens in the ceiling.

Other amusements include two roller-coasters, a water-rapid ride and a handful of others spanning the adrenaline-rush scale. All are inclusive with admission, and height restrictions apply.

Express bus no. 629 runs to the park from Admiralty MTR Station and Central Pier 7.

Ocean Park; Ocean Park Road, Aberdeen; tel: 3923 2323; www. oceanpark.com.hk; daily 10am–7pm; charge; map D3

Lantau and Outer Islands

5 Ⓔ

N

Lung
Kwu Tan

Lung Kwu
Chau

Ha Tsuen/
Castle Peak
Firing Range

Castle Peak
583

Tuen Mun

Sam
Shing Hui

Shek
Kok Tsui

Siu Lang
Shui

Castle
Peak Bay

Pearl
Island

Pillar Point

4 Ⓔ

Sha Chau
(Tree Island)

Tai Mo To

Siu Mo To

Mo To Chau
(The Brothers)

ASIAWORLD-
EXPO

AsiaWorld-
Expo

AIRPORT

proposed
border control
facility

Hong Kong
International Airport
Chek Lap Kok

Chek
Lap Kok

8

North Lantau Highway

Pak
Mong

3 Ⓔ

proposed Hong Kong – Zhuhai – Macao Bridge

San Tau

Sha Lo
Wan

Tung
Chung
Wan

Tung Chung

Ngong Ping 360

Sham Shek
Tsuen

Tai O

Lantau North
Country Park

Lo Hon
Monastery

Tung Chung
Fort

Ma Wan
Chung

Lantau North
Country Park
(Extension)

Ngau Kwu
Long

Hung Fa
Ngan

Silvermine
Beach
Hotel

Mui O

Luk Tei
Tong

Lantau
Island

Nei Lak Peak
751

Ngong
Ping

Ying Ming
Monastery

Keung
Shan

Tian Tan
Buddha
Statue

Po Lin
Monastery

Tea Farm

Tei Tong
Tsai

Lantau Peak
934

Sunset Peak
869

3

Lantau South
Country Park

Pui O
Tsuen

Pui O Beach

2 Ⓔ

Nga
Ying
Kok

O San
Tsuen

Man
Cheung
Po

Lantau South
Country Park

Shek Pik
Reservoir

Cheung Sha

Cheung Sha
Beach

Chi M
Peni

Shek Pik

Shui Hau

Tong Fuk

Tong Fuk
Miu Wan

Tai Long
Wan

Cha Kwo
Chau

Fan Lau
Sai Wan

Fan Lau

Fan Lau
Fort

Kau Ling
Chung

1 Ⓔ

Siu A Chau

Shek Kwu
Chau

Ⓐ Ⓑ Ⓒ Ⓓ

Soko Islands

Tai A Chau

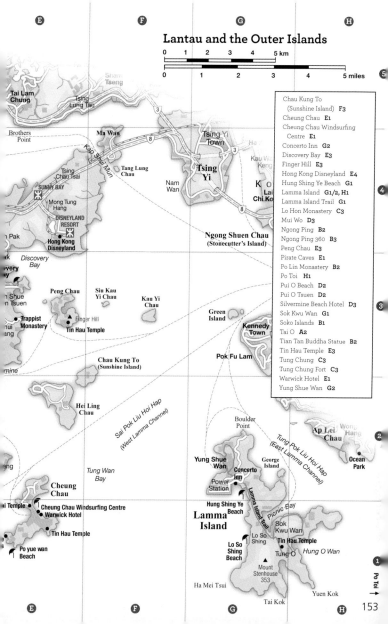

Lantau and the Outer Islands

Be humbled by the **world's tallest seated bronze Buddha** at Po Lin

the Lunar Calendar's tally with its Gregorian counterpart). The Buddha can often be glimpsed when arriving in or leaving Hong Kong by air during the daytime.

A walk in the monastery grounds is pleasant, especially on a weekday when it's less crowded; a vegetarian meal can be enjoyed in the refectory. To reach Po Lin, you can get the MTR to Tung Chung then bus no. 23 or the scenic Ngong Ping 360 cable car (*p.155*); but if time allows, it's worth getting the ferry from Central Pier 6 to Mui Wo then minibus no. 2. The views from the switchbacks are impressive, and the journey builds up the anticipation of finally seeing the Buddha.

If you're after a less-visited Buddhist retreat, a three- to four-hour hike on the Lantau Trail westward from Po Lin leads to Ginger Mountain, home to quiet, brightly painted **Tsz Hing Monastery**, with its multi-tiered rooftops. Around halfway between Tsz Hing and Po Lin, paths down to Keung Shan Road connect with Mui Wo and Ngong Ping.

At the end of a network of hairpin bends, high above most of lesser-visited Lantau Island, is the red, orange and gold **Po Lin Monastery**, presided over by the world's largest outdoor seated bronze Buddha, at 34 metres tall.

The Tian Tan deity, seated on a lotus leaf pad with a serene downward gaze, is reached by a climb up 268 steps from the monastery. Devout Buddhists from the world over visit all year – but in notably large numbers on Buddha's birthday in the summer (July or August, depending on

Po Lin Monastery; Ngong Ping, Lantau Island; tel: 2985 5248; monastery 9am–6pm, Buddha 10am–6pm, vegetarian meals 11.30am–5pm; free; map B2

Take a memorable ride on the soaring **Ngong Ping 360 cable car**

The sightseeing **Ngong Ping 360** cable-car route stretches 5.7km up the side of a Lantau mountain from Tung Chung to the Ngong Ping Plateau, a five-minute walk from the giant Buddha above Po Lin Monastery (*p.154*). This makes it the biggest cableway in Asia, and its name refers to the panorama you're treated to on board – with magnificent views across Lantau and beyond.

To further upgrade the experience, you can ride in a **Crystal Cabin**; of the 109 suspended capsules, these 36 have transparent flooring to enhance the sensation of floating. They also carry fewer passengers (10 rather than the standard 17). The ultimate first-class cabin is the eight-passenger-capacity **Sky Lounge**, designed by respected local architect Steve Leung. Laden with bling including Swarovski crystal and LED lighting, this is the one to be seen in. Free with a Sky Lounge booking, or bookable separately, is the 'Journey of Enlightenment' package, which includes a round-trip cable-car journey and admission to the two attractions at the Ngong Ping terminus. Walking with Buddha tells the story of the life of Siddhartha Gautama, the man who became Buddha, and Monkey's Tale Theatre is a retelling of the Chinese mythical classic, *Journey to the West*.

There are two restaurants up here too, as well as nature trails; it's easy to make a day of it.

Ngong Ping 360 cable car; Ngong Ping, Lantau Island; tel: 3666 0606; www. np360.com.hk; Mon–Fri 10am–6pm, Sat–Sun 9am–6.30pm; charge; map B3

Eat a **delicious lunch** with the nuns and monks of **Lo Hon Monastery**

For a sharp contrast to the bustle of Hong Kong's urban locales, turn off all mobile communications and head for a monastery. **Lo Hon Monastery** is easier to reach than others, and it can make for a particularly enjoyable lunchtime.

The monastery is perched on a hill with sweeping views across the relatively new high-rises of Tung Chung Town to a wide bay. Take a stroll through its small tiered vegetable, plant and religious sculpture gardens and prayer halls. The main prayer hall contains three shiny brass seated Buddhas and a conical tower studded with miniature bronze Buddhas, each of

which bears the name of a donor family; the tower is turned daily to bless these families.

By now you'll have worked up an appetite for a vegetarian lunch (noon–3pm). Lunch is served for parties of 10 or more on weekdays, with no number restrictions on weekends and holidays. Mock meats made of bean curd are used in some dishes. Soups vary daily, as does the vegetable selection – but everything is very tasty.

A 30-minute stroll west along Shek Mun Kap Road is tiny, ancient **Tung Chung Fort**. Wander its cannon-peppered walls and small museum, which describes how the fishing village and farmland used to look, and the marine police outpost that once kept watch for marauders.

Both sights are served by Tung Chung MTR station, then mini-bus no. 34 (get off at Shek Mun Kap for the monastery or Sheung Ling Pei village for the fort); or take the ferry from Central Pier 6 to Mui Wo, then either bus no. 3 or 13 to Lo Hon Pavilion or the fort.

Lo Hon Monastery; tel: 2988 1419; free; map C3
Tung Chung Fort; next to Sheung Ling Pei village; www.lcsd.gov.hk; Wed–Mon 10am–5pm; free; map C3

Visit the **fishing village** of **Tai O**, known for shrimp paste and its buildings on stilts

Being out on a limb on the west coast of Lantau Island has helped preserve the old fishing village of **Tai O**. Divided by a narrow tidal inlet, this ramshackle but charming low-rise village dots both banks, with narrow footpaths the only means of travelling through it.

Though partially devastated by a series of fires over several decades, many of the village's famous wooden-stilted houses remain, sitting above the sandy inlet that is fringed by some of the territory's last remaining mangrove coastline.

A weekend visit witnesses Tai O at its liveliest, when the market does a brisk trade in dried seafood, freshly caught fish and locally grown fruit. Shrimp paste (*pictured*) is a speciality: fermented with garlic, chilli and other flavourings, it is worth snapping up to pep up vegetable and stir-fry dishes. Down-to-earth seafood restaurants offer good value.

There are two small art galleries, and a dark, incense-filled temple in honour of Kwan Tai, Taoist God of War. To reach Tai O, take bus no. 1 from Mui Wo or bus no. 11 from Tung Chung.

Tai O; Lantau Island; map A2

DOLPHIN SPOTTING
Fishermen offer short dolphin-watching trips off the coast here – and boat tours to Tai O from Central often get you up close to the Chinese white variety. Registered charity **Hong Kong Dolphinwatch** (tel: 2984 1414; www.hkdolphinwatch.com) monitors the movements of this dwindling species and sensitively conducts sightings, while explaining the dolphins' habits and plight.

All aboard the **Disney train** to Hong Kong's **'Magic Kingdom'**

Long-awaited **Hong Kong Disneyland** opened in 2005 with its own specially commissioned MTR train from Sunny Bay station, some unique-to-Hong-Kong rides and a setting against a panoramic mountainous backdrop. Families with young children can easily spend a day here – and you can pack more into it with some exclusive experiences offered by adding a Silver or Gold Star Pass to the price of your admission. Good for up to four people (adults and kids over three all count), one of the greatest advantages of these packages is being discreetly whisked past queues straight onto rides by your tour host (some of the more popular ones can require 45 minutes' or more waiting time on weekends or holidays). Also included is the choice of appearing on a parade float or on stage, or a privileged private meet-and-greet session with two characters, plus some souvenirs.

Additional special events are laid on daily for pass holders – these might include animation drawing or drumming workshops, and exclusive photo opportunities with roaming Disney characters. A Silver pass lasts two hours, and Gold lasts three, leaving plenty of time to eat at the handful of Western and Asian restaurants, watch live and 3D film shows, jump on an 'Amazon River Cruise' peppered with lifelike robot animals or try yet more rides.

Originally split into four zones, the park is set to unveil its new Toy Story Land in 2011. There are two hotels at the theme park for the very keen (*p.177*).

Hong Kong Disneyland; Lantau Island; tel: 1-830 830; www.hongkong disneyland.com; Mon–Fri 10am–7pm, Sat–Sun 10am–9pm; charge; map E4

Take it easy at the **bars and beaches** of Mui Wo

One of the first things you notice when pulling into Lantau's **Mui Wo** (or Silvermine Bay) on the ferry is the open-fronted **China Bear** pub (3 Ngan Wan Road; tel: 2984 9720), from which tables spill out to the water's edge just left of the ferry terminal.

On any given evening or weekend lunchtime, expat and local regular patrons are usually up for relaxed chat and are a good source of island information. If you want to catch a live Premier League football game or other major sporting event, a TV will probably be screening it here. The pub-grub menu includes good thin-crust house pizza.

The village also has a mix of Chinese and Western restaurants. Popular Turkish joint **Behce** (Unit 19, Mui Wo Centre; tel: 2984 0222) serves satisfying meze and hot dishes like stuffed vine leaves, lamb kofte and fish kebabs. It also has a lively bar.

Away from Mui Wo stretches long sandy Silvermine Beach. It is a short bus ride to Tai O (*p.157*), Po Lin Monastery (*p.154*) or the unspoilt beaches of Cheung Sha (*pictured*) and Pui O.

Get here on the ferry from Central Pier 6; check the ferry timetable at www.nwff.com.hk.

Mui Wo; Lantau Island; map D3

Windsurf or **kite-board** off a small island that takes water sports very seriously

Hong Kong territorial waters are sprinkled with more than 230 islands. Here's a chance to launch off one of the larger ones, **Cheung Chau** – on a windsurf board. Rent a board and throw up your sail if you are already proficient, or take a lesson if you're not, at the **Cheung Chau Windsurfing Centre**.

To get there, board the ferry at Pier 5 in Central (check the timetable at www.nwff.com.hk), then once you've alighted at the Cheung Chau terminal take the shortish path that crosses the narrow populated isle – it's around a 10-minute walk. When you get to the island's main beach, **Tung Wan**, walk to the headland on the right – the centre is just behind it.

Classes plus board and wetsuit hire can be arranged for blocks of a few hours or the whole day. Kite-boarding is also available for novice level upwards; this involves the dual skill of flying a glider-like kite on a cord that pulls the rider through water on a compact board. Both sports can be taught in group or individual lessons, and around a week's notice is preferred. The centre has a restaurant, open to anyone, serving a Mediterranean menu.

Cheung Chau takes windsurfing all the more seriously since one of its own top enthusiasts, Lee Lai-shan, picked up the gold medal at the 1996 Olympic Games in Atlanta, USA. This was Hong Kong's first ever Olympic medal.

Cheung Chau Windsurfing Centre; 1 Hak Pai Road, Cheung Chau; tel: 2981 2772; www.ccwindc.com.hk; charge; map E1

Soak up the **waterfront atmosphere** or catch a festival on **Cheung Chau**

Dumbbell-shaped **Cheung Chau**, just south of Lantau, offers some good walks, fine beaches and a handful of temples dedicated to Tin Hau, Goddess of the Sea.

Cheung Chau village has a lively waterfront atmosphere. The waterfront promenade, the *praya*, is one of Hong Kong's most pleasant alfresco dining spots, especially after sunset. Head off in any direction from the ferry terminal and you will find both modern and traditional shops and restaurants. The village, around the ferry dock, is a tangle of interesting alleyways. Bicycles can be rented for around HK$30 a day, on which you could zip round most of the island's paths in a few hours.

The island is also known for throwing some of Hong Kong's most exuberant and colourful festivals; the annual showpiece, usually in May, is the exciting **Cheung Chau Bun Festival** *(pictured)*, during which the island's residents try to dispel what are known as 'hungry ghosts'. This involves a spectacular parade and a race up a tall tower covered in steamed buns.

Cheung Chau Island; map E1

PIRATE LOOT
Ruthless 19th-century plunderer Cheung Po Tsai and his crew are said to have stashed their loot in the pirate caves of Cheung Chau Island. The treasure is thought to remain undiscovered to this day, so a trip here could net you a tidy windfall. To reach the narrow vertiginous caves, turn right when you disembark the ferry and follow the coastal path for about 20 minutes. The slightly inclined route is signposted and offers fine views over the craggy shoreline. Signboards announce your arrival at the caverns.

Escape the city and head to a charming, tiny island

Pack your book and iPod and hop aboard a ferry from Central Pier 6 to the very low-rise and low-population **Peng Chau Island**. With its gentle walking paths and handful of restaurants and pubs, this is an archetypal island retreat – just half an hour from Central.

This tiny island of a little less than one square kilometre lies within sight of the northeastern shore of Lantau – from some parts of the isle you can make out Lantau's Discovery Bay. Like Lamma and Cheung Chau Islands, it has no roads but footpaths criss-cross it. You could easily see all the sights within a couple of hours, but it's worth staying longer and unravelling its low-key charms.

Like most of Hong Kong's inhabited islands, fishing was once Peng Chau's mainstay, and is still evident in the moored boats with nets on deck. The island was once a centre for small-scale industrial production, and as such, parts of the main village are not particularly attractive – but most of its small alleyways and scattered heritage buildings do have appeal.

The Tin Hau Temple on Wing On Street, very near the ferry pier, is more than 200 years old. Tin Hau, Goddess of the Sea, takes pride of place at a golden altar near a huge whale bone – an ancient offering from local fishermen.

A little southeast of the village is **Finger Hill**; the short, steep climb rewards you with panoramic views of Tsing Ma Bridge, Lantau and Lamma Islands and southwest Hong Kong Island.

Peng Chau Island; map E3

Strap on your walking shoes for a **hike** from **Mui Wo to Pui O**

An exhilarating three-hour walk on Lantau Island takes you from **Mui Wo** (*p.159*), over mountains to the fine long beach at **Pui O**. Both ends of this hike have restaurants, so you can start with a meal, end with one, or do a double dine.

This 15km or so segment of the 70km Lantau Trail rises immediately from a path at the town end of Mui Wo's Silvermine Bay, winds through woodland, then up to breezy shrub-covered hillside where ocean and mountain views abound. This section of the trail never rises much higher than around 450 metres. Make sure you bring water; there are no shops for a few hours. Looking towards the centre of the island at certain points on the undulating path, you can see its two tallest mountains, Lantau and Sunset Peaks, rising to 934 and 869 metres. They also lie on the Lantau Trail and can be climbed.

The end of this walk dips down towards the small estuary and long wide sandy stretch of Pui O. Of the few small shops and cafés, a local no-nonsense Cantonese favourite is **Mau Kee Restaurant** (tel: 2984 1151), good for hearty noodle dishes. Most enjoyable, perhaps, for a full-on beach experience is **Oh La La** (tel: 2546 3543), just off the sand and serving a Western menu. It's the perfect spot for a sundowner.

From Pui O, you could get bus no. 1 (or 7P at weekends) back to Mui Wo; or bus nos. 3 or 3M, or a taxi, to Tung Chung.

Mui Wo; map D3
Pui O; map D2

Traverse two hills, from Yung Shue Wan to Sok Kwu Wan, on **Lamma Island**

The hills, beaches and international cafés of Lamma Island, lying around half an hour away from Central, make for a perfect contrast to urban Hong Kong. **Yung Shue Wan** and **Sok Kwu Wan**, its two small ferry terminal ports, are connected by a trail that dips up and down two manageable hills. The signposted walk takes around one hour.

You can get the ferry from Central Pier 4 to either Yung Shue Wan or Sok Kwu Wan (see www.hkkf.com.hk for timetables). Yung Shue Wan, home to a multicultural mix of residents, is the most populated of Lamma Island's villages and has something of a Mediterranean feel, with flats and houses climbing up a small hill and open-sided restaurants hugging the curve of the harbour wall. There is a Tin Hau (Goddess of the Sea) temple, where offerings of incense, fruit and food are made. If you're in Yung Shue Wan before 10am, Main Street buzzes with fishermen selling their catches and makeshift stalls touting fruit and vegetables, dried herbs and seafood, and no-nonsense clothing and homeware.

Take a stroll literally through the seafood restaurants along Main Street – the sole access path cuts through eateries whose kitchens and indoor tables are on one side, and alfresco seafront tables on the other.

Like all of these, **Sampan Seafood Restaurant** (no. 16; tel: 2982 2388), the second one you reach from the ferry pier, has bubbling aquariums, packed with fish, molluscs and crustaceans. The steamed fish, stir-fried crab and dim sum are all good, as are the prices. Of the international selection, **Bluebird Japanese Restaurant's** (no. 24; tel: 2982 0687) big bowls of noodles, or set meals with sushi, hit the spot. With a bohemian air, **Bookworm Café** (no. 79; tel: 2982 4838) serves up Western-style vegetarian dishes; enjoy a hearty bean curd 'shepherdess pie', meze plate or organic salad here.

Some 25 minutes' walk from Yung Shue Wan's ferry pier, past some three-storey buildings and neat vegetable plots, **Hung Shing Ye Beach** is a good stopping point.

There is a restaurant here at the small hotel **Concerto Inn** (28 Hung Shing Ye Beach; tel: 2982 1668).

From here, follow the marked trail for a further half-hour, passing dirt paths that lead to beautiful beaches such as signposted **Lo So Shing** and to Lamma's tallest peak, Mount Stenhouse (353m).

On the way into less-populated Sok Kwu Wan, you pass a Tin Hau temple. Further on, quality seafood restaurants line the waterfront all the way to the ferry pier. **Rainbow** (16–20 First Street; tel: 2982 8100) serves up garlic prawns and lobster in 10 kinds of butter; and **Lamma Hilton Shum Kee** (26 First Street; tel: 2982 8290) is a reliable favourite. Take your pick, watch the boats come in, and, when sated, jump on one back to Central.

Lamma Island; map G1/2

Hire a junk to visit off-the-beaten-track **Po Toi Island** – or view it from the comfort of your boat

Po Toi, one of the smallest inhabited islands in Hong Kong, lies in its southernmost territorial waters. Though served by a sporadic public ferry at weekends, it makes a decent destination for chartering a junk – a small wooden pleasure boat – or a white fibreglass vessel.

These kinds of pleasure boats can come with catering, or you may opt instead to hop off and eat ashore. Prices for a day's hire start at around HK$3,800; some operators will offer half-day rates. Most boats have a few snorkel and mask sets, large rubber rings for quick dips, and a freshwater shower; often there is also a small motorised dinghy for shuttling to shore.

Junk and pleasure boat hirers with good reputations include

Sea Lagoon (Room 1801, Wing On Central Building, 26 Des Voeux Road Central, Central; tel: 2165 4196), **Saffron Cruises**, (20/F, Teda Building, 87 Wing Lok Street, Sheung Wan; tel: 2857 1311; www.saffron-cruises.com) and **Detours Limited** (17/F, Neich Tower, 128 Gloucester Road, Wan Chai; tel: 2573 5282; www.dukling. com.hk). The latter hires out a particularly characterful vessel, the red-sailed (but still motorised) *Duk Ling*, with painstakingly renovated 50-year-old decks in the same design as junks built in the mid-19th century.

You may prefer to simply view Po Toi from the comfort of your hired vessel, but if you do go ashore, the island is laced with a few dramatic coastal paths; the best leads to a stark granite headland where cliffs drop away into the surging South China Sea below. A gentler hike heads over rough internal hill trails where kites, white-bellied sea eagles and gulls fly overhead.

In the small village are a few seafood restaurants offering tasty meals with an excellent sea view; nearby there's a **Tin Hau Temple** that is more than 150 years old.

Po Toi Island; map H1

Spend Saturday night **bar-hopping** the friendly pubs in Lamma Island's **Yung Shue Wan**

Saturday night on some of Hong Kong's outlying islands can be pretty quiet. Luckily, Lamma Island's busiest village Yung Shue Wan has some great pubs – and they're all within staggering distance along Main Street.

From the ferry pier, three pubs punctuate the path. Patrons from **The Island Bar** (no. 6; tel: 2982 1376), right next to the pier, regularly clog the path on weekend evenings, when they stand outside and spill into a small public garden opposite. This most lively of Lamma pubs often has bands playing its tiny stage. You can see ferries coming in from here and be on one within a few minutes.

Most favoured by Lamma locals, **Fountain Head** (no. 18; tel: 2982 2118) has tall counters inside and street-side tables. **Diesel's Bar** (no.

51; tel: 2982 4116) is a converted traditional Chinese village house, with a small walled terrace outside. At both venues, English Premiership football games are screened live; at these times the atmosphere is pretty animated.

Two small restaurants become relaxed watering holes by around 10pm. **The Waterfront** (no. 58; tel: 2982 1168), just off the main drag, has a canopied terrace on which you can enjoy tasty pastas and cottage pie. Regulars perch at the entrance bar, where there is a selection of draught pumps. **Deli Lamma Restaurant & Bar** (no. 36; tel: 2982 1583) has a partly Indian menu – its tandoor-cum-pizza oven produces some tasty dishes. Sit waterside or in cosy indoor booths.

Yung Shue Wan; map G2

hotels

Until a decade ago, Hong Kong's most highly rated hotels appeared to be in competition with each other and their Asian neighbours for the most opulence they could muster. While a few of the best are still bedecked in fine polished marble, generous in their chandelier count and greet you with an entrance fountain, lower-key warm luxury has become more common.

Many historic colonial-era structures have long gone in Hong Kong; interestingly, you can stay in two that remain. And a handful of high-calibre hotels with a modest number of rooms have opened across the territory, making for a more personal experience between staff and guests. Several of these places are very contemporary-looking, with some of the best of local and international architects involved in their design.

Central and Causeway Bay on Hong Kong Island, and Tsim Sha Tsui in Kowloon, are the most exciting addresses to stay in to feel the city's pulse. And like elsewhere, they offer prices that range from luxury to budget.

If you prefer a quieter environment on your doorstep and don't mind a commute, consider a stay in the New Territories or on an outlying island: it makes the impact of the high-rises all the more striking.

HOTEL PRICES
Price for an average room in high
season, including breakfast

$$$$	over HK$3,000
$$$	HK$2,000–3,000
$$	HK$1,000–2,000
$	under HK$1,000

Historic Hotels

The Peninsula
Kowloon
Salisbury Road; tel: 2920 2888;
www.peninsula.com; map p.91 C1; $$$$
The grand dame of Hong Kong hotels.
Enjoy afternoon tea under its tall
rococo lobby ceiling, or sip a cocktail
with a harbour view at Felix bar and
restaurant. Try to bag a corner suite,
with modern appliances hidden in
antique cabinets, oversized bathtubs,
and brass telescopes that allow you to
take in the views.

Hullett House
Kowloon
2A Canton Road; tel: 3988 0000;
www.hulletthouse.com; map p.91 B1; $$$$
This boutique hotel in the former
Marine Police Headquarters launched
its 10 suites in May 2010. Individually
themed and each named after one of
the territory's many bays, they retain
the character of their listed interior,
while incorporating some modern
quirks. Others are more genteel and
evocative of the local early colonial era.

Mandarin Oriental
Central
5 Connaught Road; tel: 2522 0111; www.
mandarinoriental.com/hongkong; map p.25
E4; $$$$
As so few pre-1950s Hong Kong
buildings remain, this flagship hotel
easily qualifies as historic. Its compact
lobby and wooden balustraded
staircase are vintage time capsules, but
many areas were renovated around the
start of the millennium. Rooms were
enlarged and glass-walled bathrooms
also opened up the sense of space.

The Lap of Luxury

Four Seasons Hotel
Central

8 Finance Street; tel: 3196 8888; www.four seasons.com/hongkong; map p.24 D5; $$$$

Guest rooms here have tall ceilings, are bright and feel spacious. Almost at the water's edge, harbour-view rooms graze the tip of Kowloon Peninsula, as does the outdoor pool. The Chinese and French restaurants have received several awards and the lobby lounge is an unsung find for high-calibre international comfort food.

The Landmark Mandarin Oriental
Central

15 Queen's Road Central; tel: 2132 0188; www.mandarinoriental.com/landmark; map p.25 E4; $$$$

The LMO boasts some of the largest rooms in Hong Kong, and their design is particularly unusual – oval in shape with bathrooms at their centre. Despite the big name behind it, this hotel has just 113 rooms and remains boutique in feel, with a small library and a cosy spa and fitness area.

Island Shangri-La
Admiralty

Pacific Place, 88 Queensway; tel: 2877 3838; www.shangri-la.com; map p.25 G3; $$$$

The lavishness rarely stops at this place. With an intimate lobby and a fair range of restaurants, bars, an outdoor pool and fitness areas spread over the first few floors, it feels far cosier than its 550-plus rooms and suites would suggest. Room interiors are warm, and Western in feel, with oriental touches. High floors face The Peak or Victoria Harbour.

Grand Hyatt
🟦 Wan Chai

1 Harbour Road; tel: 2588 1234; www.hong kong.grand.hyatt.com; map p.70 C4; $$$$

The old-school black marble and large fountain pool remain, but rooms were given a modern makeover in the noughties. Suites are like modern apartments, often with open-plan living room and dining suite areas, and self-contained kitchens. The afternoon tea buffet at Tiffin Lounge and Champagne Bar is an indulgent treat.

InterContinental
🟦 Kowloon

18 Salisbury Road; tel: 2721 1211; http://hongkong-ic.intercontinental.com; map p.91 C1; $$$$

The InterContinental, perched right on the waterfront at Tsim Sha Tsui, has completed several phases of a luxurious modern makeover. A popular top-end business hotel, its great views, outdoor pool and luxurious spa make it a great urban leisure retreat. Rooms are understated in their elegance.

Designer Chic

JIA
🟦 Causeway Bay

1–5 Irving Street; tel: 3196 9000; www. jiahongkong.com; map p.71 G4; $$

This boutique hotel, whose name means 'home' in Mandarin, employed design guru Philippe Starck to make his mark on its 54 rooms. Cream fabrics and teak floors are backdrops to vividly coloured upholstery and eye-catching faux-rococo and contemporary furniture.

W
🟩 Kowloon

1 Austin Road West; tel: 3717 2222; www.
starwoodhotels.com; map p.91 A3; $$

Bringing Manhattan chic to the East,
W's brand of contemporary luxury is
self-consciously hip. But it remembers
to have fun, and rooms, restaurants
and bars bear quirky motifs and
sculptural forms. Rooms provide high
thread-count bed linens and oversized
writing desks, and overlook Kowloon
or Victoria Harbour.

The Putman
🟩 Sheung Wan

202 Queen's Road; tel: 2233 2233;
www.theputman.com; map p.48 D3; $$$

This designer hotel, five minutes'
walk from Central, is named after the
esteemed designer herself – French
talent Andrée Putman. Suites are light
spaces adorned with her furniture
and accessories, and are equipped
with washer-dryer machines, decent
kitchenettes, dining tables and chairs
and 42-inch TV screens.

Away From It All

Le Méridien Cyberport
🟩 Southside

100 Cyberport Road; tel: 2980 7788; www.
starwoodhotels.com; map p.138 A4; $$$

This hotel is near Cyberport's small-
town hub of two small malls of shops
and restaurants. Despite a very
contemporary lobby, compact, bright
and comfortable rooms retain a warmth
alongside iPod docks and other techie
features. Many have sea views, as does
the small outdoor pool deck.

Warwick Hotel
Outer Islands

East Bay, Cheung Chau Island; tel: 2981 0081; www.warwickhotel.com.hk; map p.153 E1; $$

Bright and comfortable rooms have tiny balconies overlooking Cheung Chau's main beach. There's an outdoor swimming pool, a small spa and beauty salon, a decent Cantonese restaurant and a café on a terrace. You can go windsurfing, sea kayaking or fishing from the beach below; or try beach volleyball or an island hike.

Concerto Inn
Outer Islands

Hung Sing Ye Beach, Yung Shue Wan, Lamma Island; tel: 2982 1668; www.concertoinn.com.hk; map p.153 G2; $

Set back off the most popular beach at the Yung Shue Wan end of Lamma, this hotel looks across the small bay to mountains in the island's south atop a cliff coastline. Rooms were renovated recently; though small, they have modern, attractive decor. A ground-floor entertainment room is fronted by a terrace restaurant and bar.

Silvermine Beach Hotel
Lantau Island

DD2 Lot 648, Silvermine Bay, Mui Wo, Lantau Island; tel: 2984 8295; www.resort.com.hk; map p.152 D3; $$

Fronted by beautiful Silvermine Bay Beach, this comfortable hotel has loads of appeal. Forget airs and graces; staff are polite and simple rooms are set around a lawn garden. All have a balcony with a garden, mountain or beach view. Larger family rooms are available.

Rooms with a View

Kowloon Shangri-La
⬛ Kowloon
64 Mody Road, Tsim Sha Tsui East; tel: 2721 2111; www.shangri-la.com; map p.91 D2; $$$$

This long-time top-end favourite has just had a staggered renovation. The marble lobby remains traditionally lavish; rooms are stylish and more understated. Floor-to-ceiling windows take in harbour views or cityscapes; suites with adjoining living and dining rooms enjoy wider vistas still.

The Upper House
⬛ Admiralty
Pacific Place, 88 Queensway; tel: 2918 1838 www.upperhouse.com; map p.25 G3; $$$$

With its lowest rooms on this tower's 38th floor, impressive harbour or city vistas are guaranteed. Designed by local award-winning architect Andre Fu, the hotel takes 'home from home' as its cue, with a private lawn garden and a warm bar, strewn with sofas and armchairs. Bar-restaurant Café Gray Deluxe offers spectacular night views.

Renaissance Harbour View Hotel
⬛ Wan Chai
1 Harbour Road; tel: 2802 8888; www.marriott.com; map p.70 C4; $$$$

Overlooking the waterfront, this hotel also has views of the adjacent bird-in-flight structure of the Hong Kong Convention and Exhibition Centre. It houses high-calibre Western and Chinese restaurants; rooms and suites are light and modern in design. An impressive large outdoor pool deck includes a shallow one for kids.

Heart of the Action

The Mira
▮ Kowloon
118 Nathan Road, Tsim Sha Tsui; tel: 2368
1111; www.themirahotel.com; map p.91
C2; $$$

This contemporary re-branding of the
old Miramar Hotel is an eye-pleaser
that offers a high level of hospitality.
Very contemporary in its lobby and
restaurant, it's less so in the rooms,
which are bright and colourful, with
warm lighting and lots of mod cons. A
place to come for reliable quality.

Langham Place
▮ Kowloon
555 Shanghai Street, Mong Kok; tel: 3552
3552; http://hongkong.langhamplacehotels.
com; map p.90 B7; $$$

There was some doubt when this slick
modern luxury hotel opened in such an
earthy neighbourhood, but naysayers
were quickly proved wrong. Luxurious
bedding, deep tubs, rainforest showers
and large flatscreen TVs all add up to a
lot of comfort. Plus there's a great spa
and a glass-walled rooftop pool.

Hotel LKF
▮ Central
33 Wyndham Street; tel: 3518 9688; www.
hotel-lkf.com.hk; map p.24 D4; $$$$

Tasteful luxurious rooms sit
above Hong Hong's most well-
known restaurant and nightlife
zone, Lan Kwai Fong – high up
and soundproofed enough to be
undisturbed by the action. Rooms
are large, each with a coffee maker
and Bulgari bathroom products. The
hotel restaurant-bar serves breakfast,
cocktail-hour drinks and canapés.

The Excelsior
🔲 Causeway Bay

281 Gloucester Road; tel: 2894 8888; www.mandarinoriental.com/excelsior; map p.71 F4; $$$

Perched above the typhoon shelter at Causeway Bay, this no-nonsense hotel's rooms are functional, if a little vintage in their decor. There's a small gym and business centre; the 34th-floor restaurant and bar Totts, Chinese restaurant Yee Tung Heen, and Italian Cammino are all excellent.

The Luxe Manor
🔲 Kowloon

39 Kimberley Road; tel: 852 3763 8888; www.theluxemanor.com; map p.91 C3; $$$

This boutique hotel incorporates unexpected surreal elements: some guest rooms feature picture-less frames that climb the wall onto the ceiling; and flat-screen TVs are edged with gilded rococo-style frames. There are six themed suites, with outlandish furniture and billowing fabrics. Italian restaurant Aspasia is well regarded.

Family Friendly

Hollywood Hotel
🔲 Lantau Island

Hong Kong Disneyland, Lantau Island; tel: 3510 5000; www.hongkongdisneyland.com; map p.153 E4; $$$

There are two onsite hotels at Hong Kong Disneyland. With an Art Deco, American retro feel, Hollywood Hotel has a piano-shaped outdoor pool and its Sunset Terrace restaurant offers outdoor barbecue cuisine. Victorian-style Disneyland Hotel is next door.

Hong Kong Gold Coast Hotel
New Territories
1 Castle Peak Road, Castle Peak Bay; tel: 2452 8888; www.goldcoast.com.hk; map p.114 B3; $$

The most comfortable beach hotel in Hong Kong, Gold Coast Resort is set in lush landscaped gardens, with large adult and kids' pools – it's a great family spot. There's also a kids' climbing wall, playground, games room and video game arcade; and for parents, a modern gym and health and beauty spa.

Value and Comfort

The Salisbury YMCA
Kowloon
41 Salisbury Road; tel: 2369 2211; www.ymcahk.org.hk; map p.91 B1/C1; $$

Next to The Peninsula hotel in Tsim Sha Tsui, and sharing the same fine view of Victoria Harbour, is The Salisbury. Don't mistake this for a backpacker hang-out – it's comfortable and clean, if a bit utilitarian. A gym, pool, beauty salon and two restaurants are all under the same roof.

The Fleming
Wan Chai
41 Fleming Road; tel: 3607 2288; www.thefleming.com.hk; map p.70 D4; $$$

Only just in this price category, rooms are essentially good value. Its contemporary interior is bright and warm. Rooms are big, with large bathrooms and flat-screen TVs. Guests have access to a decent nearby gym. Lobby-level edgy tapas restaurant Cubix doubles up as a bar.

Eaton Hotel
🔲 Kowloon

380 Nathan Road, Jordan; tel: 2782 1818; www.eaton-hotel.com; map p.91 C4; $$$$

Compact, warmly designed, modern rooms, with plenty of high-tech gizmos and friendly service, add up to a cosy, affordable winner. A rooftop swimming pool, gym and lively good-quality restaurants and bars are all pluses. It's very close to Temple Street Market and Tsim Sha Tsui. The E Club rooms get access to a privilege lounge.

Cosmo Hotel
🔲 Wan Chai

375–377 Queen's Road East; tel: 3552 8388; www.cosmohotel.com.hk; map p.71 E3; $$

Cosmo is a modern value hotel that oozes bright casual chic. Guest rooms and suites have orange, green or pastel yellow accents. Suites come in studio or two-bedroom size. Long-stay packages, of seven nights or more, offer discounts on food, beverages and laundry services. A complimentary shuttle bus accesses the main downtown districts on Hong Kong Island.

Essentials

A

Addresses
The ground floor is G/F, the one above 1/F (first floor) and so on, but address may be written '205' (for second floor, apartment 5).

B

Business Cards
In business and similar situations in Hong Kong, you will be expected to present a business card. Present cards with both hands, and accept them the same way.

C

Children
Most five-star hotels offer babysitting services.

Climate
Subtropical Hong Kong has four seasons:
Winter: late December to February; the weather varies from mild to cool, with some fog and rain; 13°C (55°F) to 20°C (68°F), occasionally dipping below 10°C (50°F).
Spring: March to mid-May; damp, overcast and pleasant sunny days; 20°C (68°F) in March to 30°C (86°F) in May. Humidity is usually high.
Summer: Hazy, humid heat, punctuated by dramatic rainstorms, alternates with clearer days; usually above 30°C (86°F), and 80–90 percent humidity day and night. July until September are peak typhoon months.
Autumn: A pleasant time to visit Hong Kong, with cooler, drier air. From late September, temperatures drop from 29°C (84°F) to around 20°C (68°F) in December.

Clothing
During the hottest months wear the lightest clothes possible and sandals. Bring a sweater or jacket for over-air-conditioned buildings. Temperatures vary sharply from one day to the next from November to April, so pack for warm and cool days, and dress in layers. Few buildings have heating, so it can seem colder inside than out.

Consulates and Visa Offices
Australia: Consulate-General, 23–24/F Harbour Centre, 25 Harbour Road, Wan Chai; tel: 2827 8881; www.australia.org.hk.
Canada: 12–14/F, Tower 1, Exchange Square, 8 Connaught Place, Central; tel: 3719 4700; www.hongkong.gc.ca.
New Zealand: 6501 Central Plaza, 18 Harbour Road, Wan Chai; tel: 2525 5044; www.nzembassy.com/hong-kong.
UK: Consulate-General, 1 Supreme Court Road, Admiralty; tel: 2901 3000; www.britishconsulate.org.hk.

USA: Consulate-General, 26 Garden Road, Central; tel: 2523 9011; http://hongkong.usconsulate.gov.

Mainland China
Office of the Commissioner of the Ministry of Foreign Affairs, 7/F, Lower Block, China Resources Building, 26 Harbour Road, Wan Chai; tel: 3413 2300 (www.fmcoprc.gov.hk). Visa applications to visit the mainland are made at the **Visa Office** (7/F). Two photos are required, and single entry visas cost from HK$250 (depending on nationality), and are processed in about three days. China visas can also be obtained through many Hong Kong travel agents.

Crime and Safety
Hong Kong has a low level of crime. In the main shopping and entertainment areas men and women can walk alone pretty safely at any hour. Tourists may be more obvious targets for pickpockets in busy areas, but normal basic precautions usually suffice.

Customs
Visitors over 18 can import almost anything for their personal use (including an unlimited amount of cash), but only 60 cigarettes (or 15 cigars/75g of tobacco) and one litre of spirits. For further details, see www.customs.gov.hk.

D
Disabled Travellers
Apart from the airport, big hotels and some newer buildings, Hong Kong is not easy for travellers with disabilities to navigate. Useful access information to public buildings and attractions is on the Hong Kong Tourism Board's website (www.discoverhongkong.com) and at its information centres. A guide to transport facilities: www.td.gov.hk. Taxis are often the easiest way to get around.

E
Electricity
Hong Kong's electrical system runs at 200/220 volts and 50 cycles AC. Sockets take British-style three-pin plugs.

Emergency Numbers
General emergencies: 999 (for police, fire service or ambulance)
Police Enquiries: 2527 7177
Hospital Authority: 2300 6555

H
Health
No vaccinations are required to enter Hong Kong, but doctors often recommend immunisations against flu and tetanus. Tap water exceeds WHO standards, but bottled water

may be more palatable and is widely available. For current information on influenza and other health concerns, see www.who.int/csr/en.

Medical Services
Hong Kong's government health care system requires visitors to pay HK$570 if they use the Accident & Emergency services at public hospitals. For information on all medical services, call the Hospital Authority helpline, tel: 2300 6555, or visit www.ha.org.hk.

Hospitals
Queen Elizabeth Hospital: 30 Gascoigne Road, Kowloon; tel: 2958 8888.
Queen Mary Hospital: 102 Pok Fu Lam Road, Hong Kong Island; tel: 2855 3838.
24-hour GP and outpatient service at **Hong Kong Central Hospital**: 1B Lower Albert Road, Central; tel: 2522 3141.

Pharmacies
Pharmacies (identified by a red cross) are abundant, as are traditional Chinese herbalists. Pharmacies will only accept prescriptions issued by a doctor in Hong Kong.

Holidays
Hong Kong's public holidays combine Chinese, Christian and, more recently, Mainland days of note. Banks, offices,

post offices and some shops are closed on the following days:
1 January: New Year's Day
Late January/February: Chinese (Lunar) New Year, a three-day holiday
March/April: Good Friday and Easter Monday
March/April: Ching Ming Festival
April/May: Buddha's Birthday
1 May: Labour Day
June: Tuen Ng (Dragon Boat) Festival
1 July: Hong Kong Special Administrative Region Establishment Day
September: Mid-Autumn Festival
1 October: China National Day
October: Chung Yeung Festival
25 December: Christmas Day
26 December: Boxing Day

Hours
Offices generally open Monday to Friday 9am–5.30pm or 6pm, but some government offices open from 8.30am–4.30pm. Many business offices also work a half day (9am–1pm) on Saturdays. Banks are generally open Monday to Friday 9am–4.30pm, and Saturday 9am–12.30pm.

Mall shopping tends to go on between 10am and 9pm, but the major shopping districts of Causeway Bay and Tsim Sha Tsui stay open later, up to 11pm. Smaller local shops open earlier, and each market differs. Most shops open every day of the year, except during the Chinese New Year public holidays.

I

ID

Hong Kong residents are required to carry ID. Visitors should carry with them a form of photo identification, such as passport, or a photocopy of it.

Internet

Most hotels charge for in-room internet service. Free Wi-fi access is becoming more widespread all the time in hotels, and the government is building a citywide free GovWiFi network. You can also access the web for free at PCs in many coffee shops.

L

Language

Hong Kong's official languages are Cantonese (predominantly) and English. Street names, public transport and utilities signage and government publications are bilingual, as are most notices and menus. Many organisations have trilingual announcements and information – Cantonese, English and Mandarin (*Putonghua*), China's 'national' language. Basic English is understood in most downtown areas.

M

Maps

The Hong Kong Tourism Board (HKTB) Information Centres carry an extensive range of maps, and give away basic ones on arrival. The General Post Office, 2 Connaught Road, has a good choice of maps and guides in its ground-floor gift shop.

Media

Newspapers and Magazines
The South China Morning Post is the dominant English-language newspaper. Tabloid-style *The Standard* is free, focuses on local business, but covers some world news. The local editions of *Time Out*, *HK* and *BC* magazines are useful for what's on, entertainment and culture-wise. Hotel bookshops, newspaper vendors at the Central Ferry Piers, Star Ferry TST and branches of Bookazine and Dymocks bookshops all have a good selection of international newspapers and magazines.

Television
The four terrestrial TV stations are ATV World and TVB Pearl in English; ATV Home and TVB Jade in Cantonese. Most programmes on the English-language stations are US shows or films; not much is produced locally in English, except news. Most hotels offer a mix of international cable and satellite channels.

Radio
Hong Kong's government radio broadcaster RTHK relays 24-hour news from the BBC World Service on its RTHK6 channel (675 kHz AM). There

are regular English news bulletins on RTHK Radio 3 (567 and 1584 kHz AM/97.9 and 106.8 mHz FM), which airs current affairs, chat shows and pop music, and RTHK Radio 4 (97.6–98.9 mHz FM), which focuses on arts and culture. Other English-language programming comes and goes.

Money

The Hong Kong Dollar is pegged to the US dollar at around US$1 to HK$7.80. In early 2010 HK dollar exchange rates were around HK$11–13 to £1 sterling or HK$9–10 to €1.

Banknotes vary slightly, being issued by HSBC, Standard Chartered Bank and the Bank of China in the following denominations: HK$1,000, HK$500, HK$100, HK$50, HK$20 and HK$10. Coins include HK$10, HK$5, HK$2, HK$1, 50 cents, 20 cents and 10 cents.

Hong Kong dollars are interchangeable with the Macau currency the Pataca (MOP), should you visit.

Changing Money and Traveller's Cheques

Traveller's cheques are accepted by banks, hotels and money-changers. The best places to change these and foreign currency are banks, which generally offer the best rates, although most will charge commission. Bank hours are Monday to Friday 9am–4.30pm, Saturday 9am–12.30pm. Money-changers and

hotels are an alternative, but can have hefty charges. Street money-changers in Tsim Sha Tsui, Causeway Bay and Wan Chai stay open late.

Credit Cards and ATMs

Major cards are accepted at most places. However, check the cash price in shops; it may be lower than for card purchases. In most markets, only cash is accepted. ATMs are plentiful.

P

Post

Hong Kong mail is fast and efficient. Stamps are normally bought at post offices, open Monday to Friday 9am–5pm, and Saturday mornings. Airmail stamps are also available at hotels, 7-11 and Circle-K convenience stores. For more information on mail services, tel: 2921 2222; www.hongkongpost.com.

T

Telephones

Coin-operated public telephone kiosks are a rarity, with most requiring prepaid cards (available at HKTB Information Centres, convenience stores and hotels) and some accepting credit cards. Many hotels charge for local calls from your hotel room.

The IDD code is 001, followed by the country code and number. Within Hong Kong, there are no area codes; numbers have eight digits.

Mobile (Cell) Phones
To avoid roaming charges, get a prepaid SIM card with a Hong Kong number and fixed number of minutes. Many phone providers, hotel business centres and convenience stores sell them.

Telephone Codes
Hong Kong from abroad **852**
Macau **853**
Mainland China **86**

Useful Phone Numbers
Hong Kong Directory Enquiries: 1081
International Directory Enquiries: 10013
International Operator/Collect calls: 10010
Hong Kong International Airport Information, in English (24 hours): 2181 0000

Time
Hong Kong is eight hours ahead of GMT and 13 hours ahead of US Eastern Time. Unlike in Europe and the US, there is no daylight saving time, so from April to October the difference is reduced to seven hours ahead of London and 12 ahead of New York.

Tipping
Most restaurants and hotels add a 10 percent service charge to bills automatically. It's common practice to round up restaurant bills to the nearest HK$10; larger gratuities are expected when no service charge has been added. Taxi fares, too, are often rounded up to the nearest dollar or two as a sufficient tip. Restroom attendants and doormen can be tipped in loose change, and HK$10–20 is enough for bellboys and room service.

Tourist Information
HKTB has information booths at the airport, some ferry piers and land crossings, offering brochures and details of events around the territory, plus day and half-day tours run by HKTB. It also provides a multilingual visitor hotline, tel: 2508 1234 (daily 8am–6pm), and a comprehensive website: www.discoverhongkong.com.

Transport
This city has an efficient, easy-to-use public transport system. Save money and time with a stored-value Octopus travel card. Over-65s and children aged under 11 travel half-fare on most transport, and under-3s travel free.

Arriving by Air
Hong Kong International Airport
at Chek Lap Kok on Lantau Island is about 34km (21 miles) from Central, Hong Kong Island. Immigration and baggage collection move swiftly.
Airport Information: tel: 2181 0000; www.hongkongairport.com.

Transport To and From the Airport
The Airport Express rail line, part

of the MTR system, is the quickest and most convenient way into town, reaching Central station in 23 minutes, with stops at Tsing Yi and Kowloon. Trains run in both directions daily, from 5.50am–1.15am. Free shuttle buses run between Central and Kowloon Airport Express stations to many hotels, Hung Hom KCR train station and the China Ferry Terminal. Passengers can check in bags at Airport Express stations, up to two hours before departure.

There are also airport buses, and **taxis** are easy to find (costing around HK$350 to Hong Kong Island and less to Kowloon).

Arriving by Sea
Cruise ships dock at the **Ocean Terminal** in Tsim Sha Tsui, right next to the Star Ferry terminal.

Getting Around: The MTR
The Mass Transit Railway (MTR) is a fast, clean, reasonably priced rail network that runs from around 6am–12.30am. Automatic machines dispense tickets or recharge Octopus cards at all stations. Everything is signposted in English and Chinese, and on-train stop announcements are multilingual. Stations have well-marked exits, identified by letters and numbers, so it's useful to have an idea of which you want; however, there are good local area maps at all stations. Information: tel: 2881 8888; www.mtr.com.hk.

Getting Around: Buses
Bus routes cover every part of the territory. Most run 6am–midnight, but some operate all night. Drivers rarely speak much English, but digital displays on most spell out stops in English and Chinese. Octopus cards or exact change must be paid on entry. You can pick up free maps of main bus routes at HKTB Information Centres.

Sixteen-seater minibuses are another option; but be cautious, as timetables are Chinese-only and stops are unannounced.

Getting Around: Trams
Trams skirt Hong Kong Island's north shore; the flat fare is paid as you get off (*see p.36*).
The **Peak Tram** is actually a funicular railway, up to the Peak Tower (*see p.39*).
Hong Kong Tramways: tel: 2548 7102; www.hktramways.com.
Peak Tram: tel: 2522 0922; www.the peak.com.hk.

Getting Around: Star Ferries
No visit to Hong Kong is complete without a trip across Victoria Harbour on the green-and-white, open-sided Star Ferry; it runs daily 6.30am–11.30pm, taking about eight minutes between Central and Tsim Sha Tsui.
Star Ferry Information: tel: 2367 7065; www.starferry.com.hk.

Getting Around: Taxis

Taxis are easy to hail on the street, outside rush hours. They come in three colours: red on Hong Kong Island and Kowloon; green taxis run in the New Territories, and blue ones on Lantau. The minimum fee for red taxis is HK$18, with extra charges for luggage placed in the car boot, booked taxis, and tunnel and bridge tolls. All fares are metered, and receipts given. By law passengers must wear seat belts. To call a taxi, tel: 2571 2929.

Ferries to the Outlying Islands

Ferries to Lamma, Lantau, Cheung Chau and Hong Kong's other islands leave from Piers 1–6 of the Central Ferry Piers, near the Star Ferry Piers in Central on Hong Kong Island. **Information:** Ferries to Lamma: tel: 2815 6063; www.hkkf.com.hk. To Cheung Chau, Peng Chau and Lantau's Mui Wo: tel: 2131 8181; www.nwff.com.hk.

Ferries to Macau and Mainland China

Turbojet (tel: 2859 3333; www.turbojet.com.hk) runs ferries 24 hours a day, 365 days a year to Macau from the Shun Tak Centre's Macau Ferry Terminal, west of the Central Ferry Piers, and China Ferry Terminal in Tsim Sha Tsui, Kowloon – from where it also sails to ports in Mainland China. Cotai Jet (www.cotaijet.com.mo) ferries run from the same locations in Hong Kong to the ferry terminal at Taipa.

Trains to the New Territories and Mainland China

The MTR network includes four lines serving the New Territories. Trains are fast and frequent. Information: tel: 2881 8888; www.mtr.com.hk.

Several daily trains run from Hung Hom station in Kowloon to Guangzhou via Shenzhen. There are also long-distance trains to Beijing or Shanghai every two days. If direct tickets to Guangzhou are sold out, take the East Rail line to the border at Lo Wu. Shenzhen station is a few minutes' walk.

V

Visas

Most visitors only need a valid passport to enter Hong Kong. British citizens with full UK passports are given six months; nationals of other EU countries, Australia, Canada, New Zealand, the US and some other countries get three months. Hong Kong Immigration website: www.immd.gov.hk.

W

Websites

Hong Kong Tourist Board: www.discoverhongkong.com.
Hong Kong SAR Leisure and Culture Department: www.lcsd.gov.hk.
Macau Tourist Office: www.macautourism.gov.mo.

Index

Insight Select Guide: Hong Kong
Written by: Andrew Dembina
Edited by: Tom Stainer
Layout by: Ian Spick
Maps: James Macdonald
Production: Linton Donaldson
Picture Manager: Steven Lawrence
Series Editor: Cathy Muscat
Photography: All photos by APA Alex Havret
except: 4 Corners 74, 119; Alamy 26, 40, 45, 60, 103,
110, 111, 133, 162, 167; Courtesy Aqua Spriti 104;
Courtesy Atelier de Joël Rubichon 37; AWL Images
131; Courtesy Blue Bar 29; Courtesy Bo Innovation
8; Carmen 4; Courtesy Cosmo Hotel 179; Gary
Choi 52; Janine Cheung 101; Corbis 166; Courtesy
Disneyland Hotel and Theme Park 17, 158, 177B;
Courtesy The Drop 51; E Hoba 178T; Courtesy Four
Seasons 168/169, 170T; Fotolia 42/43, 63; Getty
Images 65, 68, 75, 81; Courtesy Grey Cafe Delux
35; Courtesy Hong Kong Police Museum 86; Hong
Kong Tourist Board 4/5, 8B, 31, 39, 59, 64, 66, 83,
88, 98, 107, 108, 122, 123, 135, 144, 155, 157, 161, 164,
174T; Imagine
China 9; Courtesy Isola 28; iSquare 93; iStockphoto
13, 80, 106, 120, 132, 140, 150, 160, 163; Courtesy
Jockey Club Kau Sai Chau 116; KayakandHike.com
11; Leonardo 16, 96, 170T, 172M/T, 176M/T, 177M,
178B/M, 179T; Courtesy Jia Hotels 172B; Kenneth
Lim 56; Mandarin Oriental 44, 84, 170, 171M, 177;
Courtesy Meridian Hotels 173B; Milivache 134;
Ngchikit 118; Courtesy OVOlogue 77; Pictures
Colour Library 61, 142; Photolibrary 76, 87, 102, 117;
Courtesy the Press Room 50; APA Ryan Pyle 33;
Courtesy Renaissance Hong Kong Harbour View
175B; Grischa Rueschendorf 54/55; Courtesy Shan-
gri La Hotels 171B, 176B; APA Sinopix 97; Sinopix
121; Courtesy Sky Shuttle 67; Courtesy Star St Pre-
cinct 79; Courtesy Starwood Hotels 173T; Stockfood
73, 126; Superstock 141; Toast 58; Courtesy Upper
House 175M; Paul Wan 127; David Wood 112.

First Edition 2010
© 2010 Apa Publications GmbH & Co.
Verlag KG Singapore Branch, Singapore.
Printed by CTPS-China

Distribution:
Distributed in the UK and Ireland by:
GeoCenter International Ltd
Meridian House, Churchill Way West, Basingstoke,
Hampshire RG21 6YR; tel: (44 1256) 817 987; email:
sales@geocenter.co.uk

Distributed in the United States by:
Langenscheidt Publishers, Inc.
36–36 33rd Street 4th Floor, Long Island City, New
York 11106; tel: (1 718) 784 0055; email: orders@
langenscheidt.com

Distributed in Australia by:
Universal Publishers
1 Waterloo Road, Macquarie Park, NSW 2113;
email: sales@universalpublishers.com.au

Distributed in New Zealand by:
Hema Maps New Zealand Ltd (HNZ)
Unit 2, 10 Cryers Road, East Tamaki, Auckland
2013; email: sales.hema@clear.net.nz

Worldwide distribution by:
Apa Publications GmbH & Co. Verlag KG
7030 Ang Mo Kio Ave 5, 08-65 Northstar @ AMK
Singapore 569880; tel: (65) 570 1051;
e-mail: apasin@singnet.com.sg

Contacting the Editors
We would appreciate it if readers would alert us to
outdated information by writing to:
Apa Publications, PO Box 7910, London SE1 1WE,
UK; email: insight@apaguide.co.uk

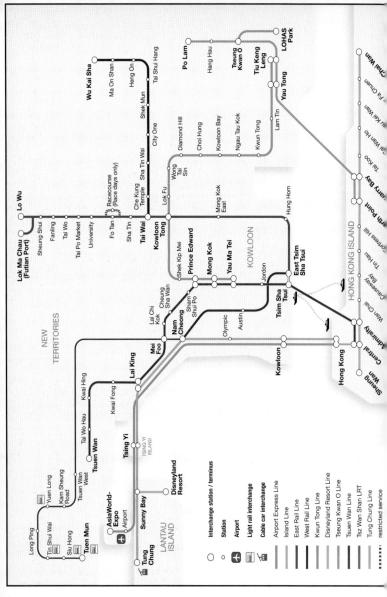